MW00886331

Hope RX'D

A collection of inspirational stories
of people finding strength
and hope through the
Functional Fitness Community

Created and Compiled by
Kelly Anne Graham

All rights reserved. No part of this publication may be reproduced, distributed, or transmitted in any form or by any means, including photocopying, recording, or other electronic or mechanical methods, without the prior written permission of the author, except in the case of brief quotations embodied in reviews and certain other non-commercial uses permitted by copyright law.

Copyright © 2015 by Kelly Anne Graham

Cover design by: Kelly Donaldson

Table of Contents

Testimonials

"HopeRX'D is an entertaining, yet powerful book full of wisdom, insight and inspiration. It is an impressive reminder that the main ingredient for growth and positive change is hope. It should be read, reflected upon and read again."

SCOTT THORNTON
NHL Player, 1989-2008
Battle of the Blade Champion, 2013
Founder of UG Series, Functional Fitness Competitions
Founder of CrossFit Indestri, Collingwood ON

"HopeRX'D is an anthology of honest, heartfelt stories that will leave you feeling all is possible. This is a book you will want to share."

MIKE KEENAN
NHL Head Coach / General Manager, 1984-2009
Stanely Cup Champion - New York Rangers, 1994
KHL Champion, 2014

"Kelly Graham's new book, HopeRX'D, is the quintessential collection of true life stories of people overcoming their own obstacles through grit and growth resulting in personal triumph. I believe this book has the power to transform each of us into the athlete we need to be."

DR JOSEPH PELINO DC BSc DACBSP
Official Chiropractor of the National Hockey League Alumni Association
Race Director for the Ironman World Championships Physically Challenged and Former NBA & NHL Team Doctor

Preface

By Kelly Anne Graham

This book would not be possible without the trust, support, and effort of so many people.

Each story submission is a clear indication that life is good and worth fighting for, that the world is full of wonderful people, that things do not go as planned and what is around that corner may be fulfillment in a way that is completely unexpected.

Thank you from the bottom of my heart to every author in this book. I was brought to tears many times while reading their stories, not because I pitied them, but was in awe of their strength and determination.

Some stories will speak to you more than others. The beauty of this collection is that it is so varied.

You will read personal accounts, laid out for all to see. Each contributor has left themselves vulnerable in order to help and inspire others. Time and time again I was told by these contributors that they felt uplifted—knowing they could possibly help people facing difficult situations.

My family is my constant and I could not have worked my way through this new, exciting, yet sometimes overwhelming experience of creating a book without them.

My husband has developed the uncanny ability to quietly support me in the most effective way.

Goal setting and commitment has always been my thing. For me, that is a blessing and a curse. I am either 110% "in" or not "in" at all. I get the job done, but sometimes at a cost. Ed (my husband) manoeuvres the land mines beautifully.

I often joke that he was the real victim in my injury. It has been, at times, a hard year and Ed has let me work through my physical and emotional recovery in such a supportive way.

One look at my three amazing children and I am quickly reminded of what is truly important in life. Sarah, Carlie, and Brett, you are my greatest blessings.

I hope you enjoy this book. It is a work full of love and hope from all over the world.

"Still I Rise"
Maya Angelou

Foreword

Many people do not live the life they truly desire because of limiting beliefs that they place on themselves as to what they can and cannot achieve. I have made it my life's mission to inspire and empower people to live the life of their dreams, no matter what setbacks, fears or roadblocks they may be facing.

Kelly Graham is also one of those people. She has been intensely involved in discovering and living her life's purpose and passion. She has done this through decades of coaching, teaching, and mentoring thousands of people to be the best they can be.

In this amazing book, Kelly shares her own inspiring story of turning tears to triumph. She also shares the stories of others, whom on their journey through life, have faced setbacks and roadblocks that would seem impossible for many to overcome.

These contributors have demonstrated the

strength of the human spirit and the power of community to not only deal with these challenges, but to grow, adapt, and move forward in a positive way.

I am grateful to have the opportunity to fly all over the world, and each time I depart, I am in awe of the potential and power these jets have to take-off to great heights with the weight they must carry.

A jet is strong, powerful, and unlimited in how far it can go and what it can achieve. If that same jet were to have no fuel, then it just sits on the runway, going nowhere...

This wonderful book shares similar ideas with us. We, as human beings, are the same as a jet — we have unlimited power and potential — provided that we have the proper fuel!

Let the stories in this book be the fuel that will set you on your runway and take you to greater heights in your own life.

Kelly, I thank you for writing this book and I am

grateful to have you as a friend. Your generosity of spirit in striving to help others find their way is contagious and so needed in this world.

Ever Onwards,

Forrest Willett | Author — #1
Bestseller "Baseball's Don't Bounce"
www.forrestwillett.com

Story One

Kelly Anne Graham

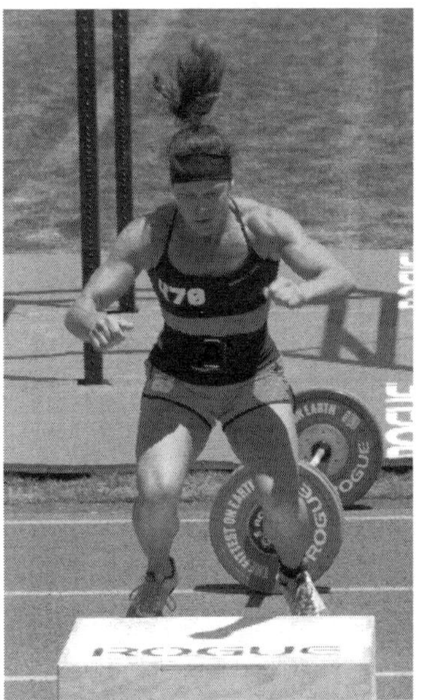

Health and fitness have always been a very important part of my life. I cannot remember a time that I was not challenging myself physically, pushing my body and training my mind to go to that dark place in order to perform at the highest level.

Determination, passion and drive are some of my greatest strengths, but they have also been characteristics that I have had to learn to control.

I have done some soul searching over the last year to try and figure out why I was not satisfied until I was the best I could be at any given pursuit, regardless of the toll it took on my body.

Interesting stuff, this self-reflection, but more on that later...

About three years before starting CrossFit, I suffered a compression injury in my lumbar spine, causing two disc bulges. This has left me with weakness and discomfort in my lower back. CrossFit helped me strengthen my core, and with the help of various therapies, I was able to excel and deal with the underlying aggravation.

I believe this initial damage to my spine has been the root of my athletic undoing.

I walked into Driven Athletics, home to Huronia CrossFit, in late August, 2012, for my first CrossFit class. Six months later, I competed in The Open, not really understanding the importance of this worldwide competition.

I finished 58th in the world in Master's Women 44-49. I already loved the sport of CrossFit and the community at my box, but now I was really hooked. My goal became to make it to the CrossFit Games in the summer of 2013.

My training continued to be the daily Work Out of the Day (WOD) at the box, but now I was determined to better my Olympic Lifting. I made some nutritional changes, falling more in line with the Paleo diet.

By Christmas of 2012, I realized I needed to ditch alcohol as well. As hoped, at the end of The Open and the Easter Weekend qualifying workouts, I was ranked 20th in the world in my division, and heading to the CrossFit Games.

At 49, I was the oldest gal in my group, but at the end of the week in Carson, California, I had earned 10th place among the fittest women in the world. I was determined that the following year I would be on the podium in first, second, or third, and I am still convinced I would have been...

Upon returning from the Games, you can imagine the even greater drive I had to train and conquer WODs, lifts and PR's. However, on Thanksgiving weekend, things began to unravel. I became severely hobbled by plantar fasciitis in my left foot, and two days later, it was in my right foot as well.

I now realize that the disc injuries in my lower back were creating tension in my fascia over time. I spent the fall and winter chasing treatments and training off my feet, hitting the pool and concentrating on upper body strengthening. I was not giving up—this was to be my year!

By the time the 2014 Open came around, I was healed enough to complete each WOD and recover before the next week. At the end of the qualifying workouts, I was ranked first in Canada and 7th in the World in Masters Women 50-54.

On top of the plantar fasciitis, I was beginning to feel some pain in my left armpit. I mentioned it to my physiotherapist and chiropractor, but we all felt (hoped?) it was trigger point or muscle tension related.

No one knew how serious things were about to get; after all, I was performing better than ever.

I continued training and was set to compete with my team at the Eastern Canadian Regionals. I was so proud and excited to represent my gym and be on this team with such amazing people. These were my role models and my trainers. I was packed up and ready to leave for the competition the next morning.

At about 3:00am, I awoke in incredible pain; my left trap, shoulder, arm and hand were on fire, and all I could do was roll around on the ground in the basement and try to stay quiet until 6:00am, when my husband woke up.

I decided I would make a pleading call to my physio to try and get in. I had no idea what was happening. As it turned out, I had suffered a large disc bulge in C 3-4 and a disc extrusion in C 5-6.

It is now over one year later and I am still waiting to see a surgeon...

Competing at Regionals was impossible and attending the Games was out of the question as well. I was devastated. I was told by the attending doctor that I was not to consider myself an elite athlete anymore. Further to that, I was told to be aware of the signs of depression, as that can happen to elite athletes when they are no longer athletes.

The nerves involved control of my diaphragm and therefore my breathing, so I really had to think hard about what my training would look like in the future. I certainly did not want to risk further or more serious damage. This message, coupled with the pain, morphine, lack of sleep and disappointment of watching my Games competition vanish, really sent me in a tailspin.

Don't get me wrong, I often had internal dialogues, reminding myself that there were so many people worse off than myself, but because my family was safe, happy and healthy, this loss was able to take over and become a very Big Deal.

I identified very strongly with being an elite athlete and role model, especially for girls and women. I would look at the parts of my arm and my back that had hollows where muscle used to be. The nerves were so damaged from the disc impingements that the muscles just sank.

I was struggling with how I saw myself and how others would see me. If I am no longer an elite athlete, what am I now? Foolish, I know, but if I am going to tell my story, I am going to be honest.

The first turning point came months later when I headed down my road for my first slow jog, which resembled more of a shuffle. I was determined to stay moving and hoped my neck could handle it.

My new neighbour, Forrest, was outside his house. We knew each other by name but had never had a real conversation. For some reason on that day, I turned up his driveway. We made small talk and all was well until he asked me how I was.

The tears came as I explained my situation in detail.

Forrest himself had suffered a devastating brain injury and multiple bodily injuries as a passenger in a car accident about 12 years ago. He had to relearn the most basic functions again.

Forrest suffered years of depression and has fought his way back to being a vibrant, successful, engaging person. I was embarrassed for being so upset over an injury so minor compared to his. He listened, hugged me, provided encouragement and never judged me.

Forrest is a motivational speaker, life coach, and bestselling author. He told me to call him day or night if I needed to talk.

A few weeks later, he knocked on my door with a signed copy of Jack Canfield's book, "*The Success Principles*." I started to read this book and could not put it down.

The very first principal spoke strongly to me. Jack opened my eyes to help me see that even though I could not control my injury, I could control how I reacted to it and that would determine the outcome. I could sit around feeling sorry for myself or I could take charge of my life again.

Jack also encouraged me to set lofty goals, just like I had been doing all my life, but at the end of each statement, add the words "or something better." This made total sense to me. So I set the goal of making it back to the CrossFit Games, but my "or something better" was to create a book to help others, just like *The Success Principles* had helped me.

I knew I wanted to remain engaged in the CrossFit community. Part of my sadness was from not knowing how I was going to maintain my strong connection to this sport that I loved and with the people in this community that I loved.

I began putting the word out that I was collecting inspirational stories about people finding strength through Functional Fitness. Slowly stories began to come in. I was lucky enough to have a few people believe in me and this project and they helped me get the word out through their established internet presence.

My husband and I spent hours upon hours emailing over 1000 CrossFit gyms in search of stories. I was honoured with accounts written by people from around the world who opened their hearts and bared their souls.

My intention was to help others who may be struggling and in the end, story by story, I was being healed as well.

I have grown a lot over the last year. I realize I loved the attention my success brought me; as tiny as my little spotlight was, I loved it. Sure I worked hard and my life was extremely disciplined, but that didn't bother me, it was worth it.

The sport, for me, had become about me. Now I see what is truly great about the CrossFit community. My bucket list has changed. I want to meet these authors and soak up the strength and passion each one of them has. I want to hug them and say "thank you for trusting me."

I want to help people gain physical and emotional strength through functional fitness. I hope to be that role model again, but this time as an example of meeting unexpected challenges, picking up the pieces when things don't go as planned, and steering your life in a positive direction.

Gratitude is a term that I didn't pay much attention to before. Through this journey I have come to realize not what I don't have, but what I do have.

*****

Kelly is a level 1 CrossFit Trainer at Driven Athletics. She recently retired from 26 years of teaching and looks forward to continuing to collect and share inspirational stories.

For more information or if you have a story to share, contact her at her websites: KellyAnneGraham.com or HopeRXD.com, or connect with her via Facebook: Kelly Graham-Athlete

Instagram: @kellygraham_xfit

Story Two

Jenny LaBaw

Adversity...Obstacles...Hardships...Misfortunes... Whatever you want to call it, life hands us situations that may divert us from our ideal path. I like to look at these as opportunities. Opportunities to grow. Opportunities to discover. Opportunities to inspire.

These opportunities come in all shapes and sizes. They may be directly or indirectly related to you. They may be internal or external. No matter how big or small they may seem, in my opinion, the way they impact your life is greatly related to your mindset.

You may be thinking, *"Oh great, she's going to get all hocus pocus on me now."* Far from the truth! Instead, I am going to share with you some of the situations that life has handed me and explain my journey in realizing these were opportunities to move forward rather than walls to hold me back.

Opportunity One: Inspire Others

When I was eight years old, I was your average young Colorado girl, climbing mountains with my family, riding bikes with my friends, and of course, aspiring to be just like my older brother, Luke, in everything that I did.

At recess one day I was swinging around the bars and all of a sudden, lost control of my right arm and went smashing to the ground. I didn't know what happened and, very embarrassed, I quickly jumped up and acted as though nothing had occurred.

After this happened a few more times, I told my parents. Obviously concerned, they made an appointment for me to go see the doctor...and then another doctor and another and another, until finally I was diagnosed with epilepsy.

What? Epilepsy! What does this mean?

Well, according to the doctors and statistics, it means I won't be able to drive, I won't be able to have children, I will be on medication the rest of my life, and this is something I was going to have to learn to live with.

They were right, to an extent...I was going to have to live with epilepsy. What they weren't right about was how it was going to affect me.

In the 25 years since I was diagnosed, I have played every school sport I could (including softball, soccer and track at the collegiate level). I graduated college with a BA in Fitness and Wellness.

I have run marathons and half marathons, I have been driving since my 16th birthday, I have trekked in the backcountry, and I have traveled internationally.

I have lived a normal life.

Now, I'm not going to pretend this journey has been full of peaks and no valleys. There were years of struggling with medication side effects, trying to find adequate dosages and combinations to stabilize my seizures, long hospital stays, and probably the worst for a young girl...the embarrassment of being different.

There was sadness, anger, hate, resentment, and pity at times. But overall, with the love and support of my family, I have conquered epilepsy.

For years I was afraid to share my story. But, with the support of my family and loving boyfriend, I had the courage to let the world know.

I had started to develop a name for myself in the CrossFit community as a Games athlete. In May of 2012, we released this short film of me telling my story: https://www.youtube.com/watch?

v=Lc7yHtLTWlA

This was the beginning of me realizing how I could make epilepsy an opportunity. Whatever fear I once had about sharing my story, it has been buried by the outpouring of responses I have received since this video.

Emails, Facebook messages, phone calls, etc. from families going through similar struggles that I went through. I have been able to give them an empathetic shoulder to cry on and words of encouragement. I have been able to help educate people on what epilepsy really is. I have been able to give others hope.

Opportunity Two: Mental Toughness

I mentioned briefly in the last section something about my CrossFit career. To give you a brief history, in 2010 I heard about CrossFit through some friends and decided I would try it out.

From what people said, I had potential to do well at it. So I then made the decision to train for my attempt at making the 2011 CrossFit Games. As luck (and a hell of a lot of hard work) would have it, I did just that.

Once at The Games, I had the experience of a lifetime, made lasting friendships and ended up surprising myself and others by coming out with a 6th place finish. This lit the fire.

Feeling strong, motivated and ready to prove to

myself I could win the whole show, I took sail for training for 2012.

In January 2012 I had a weird neck spasm that left me out of training for a week. After some bodywork and a little rest, I hit it hard again. My neck felt great and my body felt strong.

Then, in April, I had a few more flare ups that left me a bit concerned — there was something bigger that needed to be addressed.

When the MRI results came back and showed a bulging C4-C5 disc, I didn't question if I could keep training, I questioned how I was going to have to modify to keep training but also heal.

With the help of Kelly Starrett and CJ Martin, I did it. I trained around an injury for a few more months before heading into the 2012 NorCal Regionals.

I felt strong, despite not really having done much overhead work in months. Once again, I surprised myself and fought through the weekend, earning myself another spot to the Reebok CrossFit Games with a first place finish.

Spending the next couple of months with modified training, I headed to The Games feeling strong. As luck would have it, on Saturday, I was given another "opportunity."

My neck flared up during warm-ups for a handstand

pushup event. The rules stated I needed to get at least one rep to be able to get a score for the workout and continue into the weekend. So I headed out on the arena floor, did the first set of Med Ball Cleans, and carried the Med Ball 100 feet down to the handstand pushup wall. I kicked into the handstand, carefully lowered myself down and... nothing. My triceps wouldn't fire.

I told my judge what had happened and I cheered on the other athletes as they completed the event. Obviously, with a low score, my placing drastically fell on the leaderboard. I made the decision right then and there, that I wouldn't look at the leaderboard and now I was just in it to have fun and do what I could.

The next day, Saturday morning, I was able to compete in two more events and then, upon assessing the third event for the day, I had to call it. I had to make a decision based on my health, not based on what my heart thought I could/should do.

I could have easily thrown in the towel the moment my neck flared up, but instead I did what I could, without causing more harm. I then had the strength to quit (yes, this is a strength in this case) on something I had trained so hard for.

The 2012 Games wasn't the end of the neck battle. I took 2013 off from competing (see Opportunity Three), but in 2014 I trained hard, but smart around my neck. I earned a spot to the 2014 NorCal Regionals again.

The first two workouts were three attempts to get a max Snatch and then Max Distance Handstand Walking. Both of these movements flare my neck up time and time again, but feeling good going in, I had to set the intention that I was going to have a strong, healthy weekend.

This time, the power of intention wasn't quite powerful enough. On my first snatch attempt, my neck started to spasm and from there on, it was a battle all weekend. My handstand walk got cut short because I veered out of my lane due to my right triceps not being able to fire (same as in the 2012 Games). This was the beginning of a long battle all weekend.

I made it through all the workouts that weekend... wall balls, ring dips, overhead squats, muscles up and more...all with a flared up neck and weak right arm. Finishing 8th overall for the weekend, my season ended that Sunday, taking away my chance at standing on the Games floor again.

It was an emotional weekend, to say the least. To know that you are capable of so much more but are being held back because of an injury is one of the toughest things an athlete can face...something that is totally out of your control.

What can I control though?

I can control the way I let it affect my mindset. I can control what I do to intelligently progress and not regress with my neck injury. I can control the opportunities I choose to see from these cards I've been dealt.

The outcome of this opportunity is different than my epilepsy. Rather than a chance to inspire others, this was a chance to test my mental toughness.

Opportunity Three: Find Your Truth

In 2013, I was on a mission to come back from having to withdraw from the 2012 CrossFit Games. Working around my neck injury all year, I was feeling strong and encouraged.

The day before the Open, I was doing what I do on a regular basis, riding my bike home from work. I saw a man on a bike ahead of me cross my path into a parking lot on my right. I just kept pedaling along, when all of a sudden the man turned around and crossed back over my path and I T-boned him. In what seemed like slow motion, I did what any athlete would do. As I was sailing over my handlebars, I tried to bring my legs back underneath me and land on my feet. As I landed I heard a pop and felt this horrible pain in my foot.

Sparing you from all the details from the crash to the diagnosis, it turned out I had broken my foot. I remember laying in the parking lot, yelling, *"I broke my foot!"* and thinking, *"Not another year out."*

With five days until I had to have the first workout submitted, I talked to my medical support team, my family and my coach and decided that I might as well try to still get through the workouts, even if on one foot.

So for the five weeks of the Open, I waited to do the workout until the last day to give myself as much healing time as possible. In those five weeks, I shocked myself and the CrossFit community with what I was able to complete on one foot with a heavy walking cast on the other.

Snatches, double unders, muscles ups, thrusters, etc… Each week when the workouts were released, it was almost like a game for my boyfriend and me to come up with strategies for how I was going to complete the workout. There was something to almost look forward to each week because of this.

I will never forget after that final rep on the final workout on the fifth week—it hit me that I was done. My season had literally and figuratively been broken and was over.

What did I learn from this? This opportunity gave me the ability to reassess my "why." Why do I do what I do?

I do this for the challenge, for my health, and because

it's fun. But this freak accident made me find my truth. I do this because I get to inspire others all over the world everyday to be better than they were the day before, no matter what life throws at them.

I don't have to be on the podium to do that.

Throughout life we will have endless amounts of "opportunities" to become the best version of ourselves... take advantage of them. Recognize them, embrace them, and charge ahead. *"One Moment, One Chance, Always."*

*****

Jenny has taken this year to recover her body/injuries and get back some of the life an elite athlete must sacrifice to be their best. Her plan is to continue to compete at some capacity, but she is enjoying dedicating her time and energy to her work as a strength and conditioning coach, "mom" to her two yellow labs, and girlfriend to her loving boyfriend.

She has plans to become more involved with Epilepsy advocacy in the near future as well.

(Jenny's mountain photo courtesy of Marcus Brown)

Story Three

Bubba McCants

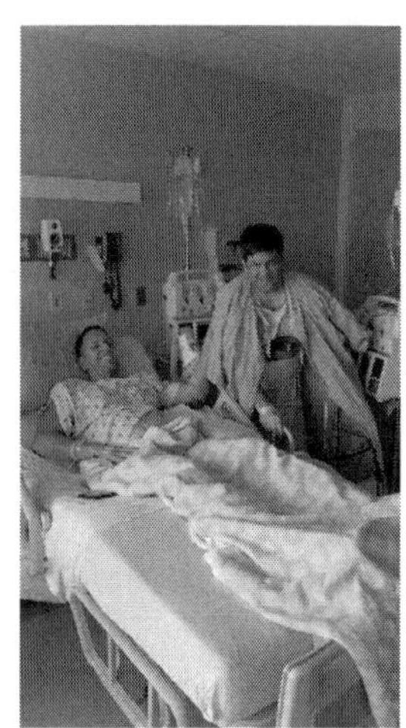

I was born and raised in Panama City. I have lived most of my life in Panama City Beach, leaving a few times for college but always coming back.

I initially met Charlie at the First Baptist Church, a long time ago. We were just kids. I was three when my family joined that church, and two years later, Charlie's family joined. Each of us remembers the other in our childhood memories.

Charlie also grew up in Panama City. He then went to

the University of South Alabama in Mobile, met his wife and has remained there for the past twenty something years.

Charlie was born with one kidney and lived a normal life as much as possible. His kidney function was routinely monitored by a nephrologist. He lived his life not ever thinking about needing a transplant; he just knew he had one kidney and carried on.

As Charlie got older, his kidney function started to deteriorate. A person with two healthy kidneys will function at an 80-100% level. Charlie was down to 10% function on his one and only kidney.

A person can live with one healthy kidney, but Charlie's was becoming less and less effective.

I hadn't seen Charlie for many years. One day I was looking through Facebook and saw a post which read "Help Find a Kidney for Charlie!" I had a vague recollection that Charlie only had one kidney from when we were growing up.

As soon as I saw it, I said, "What the heck?" Immediately, I called him. We were buddies that grew up together, but we hadn't really kept in touch. So I called him and said, *"What's up? What's going on?"* He told me about his kidney condition and I said, *"Who can try out?"* I didn't know what to ask. He said anybody.

Charlie told me what to do, and then I made a phone call. The first series of tests were blood and urine, to find out if our blood types were compatible, and they were. I was confident that I would pass any tests, both physical and mental. After all, I had been a dedicated CrossFitter for a few years.

From here there were other, more extensive tests and finally I was given the news that my kidney would be a good match for Charlie. I was so happy.

I had prayed for guidance that I was doing the right thing; I prayed that I would be given the opportunity to help Charlie. I was in total peace with this news and knew I would carry through with the procedure.

When I told my parents that I was going to donate a kidney to Charlie, my Mama's initial reaction was (I could tell by her face), *"Oh my gosh, what's my son doing?"* My dad's reaction was, *"What's my wife thinking about what her son is doing?"*

As they became more knowledgeable about the process and as I shared more about what I had learned and we all prayed about it, my family became at peace with my decision.

I'm sure lots of people wondered about the "what ifs," the things you don't know that could happen, but I didn't. I knew I was going through with this donation right from the beginning.

When Charlie was told that I was a match and that I had given consent to make the donation, he didn't know how to react. He had created the Facebook post hoping to bring awareness to the need and to basically seek anyone that would be willing to see if they would be a match. Several people did the initial blood test but I was the first one that was a true match.

Once they found out I was a match, they didn't test anyone else.

The medical team wanted to follow one person through each stage. I met with the surgery coordinator, nurse, two doctors, the surgeon, a dietician, and a psychiatrist (that was fun, she wanted to stay longer). They did an MRI and a renal arteriogram. I had to get two big jugs from a local lab and use the restroom in those for two solid days. I had two weekends where I was just going in the jug. I even took them to church. I had them in my little Alabama cooler, toting them around.

The surgeons, doctors and nurses were all very pleased with my overall health. My resting heart rate was 46 bpm and my blood pressure was 108/58. My mental strength was outstanding, measured only by me and due to the CrossFit way, I would not stop pushing and fighting until I made this kidney transplant possible.

Finally, I was told that I was accepted as Charlie's

donor.

When I called Charlie, he was obviously excited; however, he had some mixed feelings. I was someone he had known his whole life, which complicated things a bit. He had connections with my parents and worried about what if something bad happened during surgery.

Charlie was grateful that somebody was willing to do it, but at the same time he was fearful if something did go wrong, how was that going to impact everyone? Those were the kinds of things going through his mind.

The surgery occurred at the Tulane Medical Center in the abdominal transplant center on March 18, 2015. It took approximately five hours. The day before the surgery, I dropped into the Big Easy CrossFit in New Orleans. Incredibly, I worked out alongside a young medical student who just happened to be shadowing my surgeon the next day! If that wasn't a sign from above, what would be?

I never worried that things would not work out. People would applaud me for my generosity and bravery, but I truly felt that being born a healthy person with two working kidneys was a blessing from the Creator. The kidneys were really not mine, but gifts from God. I was doing God's will. I felt from the beginning that this was what I was put on this earth to do.

I have been changed for the better through this process. I don't want people to think I am some super Christian, but I am now 200% closer in my walk with Jesus.

I have been and continue to be a member of Battleship CrossFit. Like all CrossFitters, I was awaiting the 2015 Open as a way to test my mental and physical strength. After signing up, I was given the surgery date and it landed in the middle of the Open. I wanted to complete as many workouts as possible to post scores and be able to look back the following year. I completed 15.1, 15.2, and 15.3.

The community of Battleship had become like family, and I felt their love and support through this whole process. While I was on the operating table undergoing surgery, the WOD of the day was on the white board with my name attached. It was a 500 meter row buy in, followed by three rounds of 15 box jump overs, 20 pull ups, and 25 kettlebell swings.

On March 31, Battleship CrossFit hosted a Hero WOD in my honor, welcoming all athletes from any gym community to participate. Although I am certainly honored and touched by this type of outpouring, I know that I am not a hero.

Charlie has lived his whole life with one kidney. He had gone through so much and was still a wonderful father to his three children and adoring husband to his wife. Charlie maintained such a positive attitude regardless of his condition and prognosis. I am blessed to have been a part of God's plan for Charlie.

The mental and physical fortitude I developed through CrossFit played a key role in my recovery. I would not quit and I knew each day would be better than the last. The community at my box, the workouts, the PR's, the heat, every drop of sweat helped and made a difference.

CrossFit helps with what we see: the strength, the muscle, the improvements, and it also helps with what we do not see: the attitude and the mental, emotional, and spiritual strength. I am more proud to have PR'd the last four than any other.

I was told that I would not be able to return to training for 8 to 12 weeks post surgery. On April 27, I put on my colourful knee socks and Nanos and returned to Battleship for the first time.

There is a great need for organ donation. Filling out an organ donor card is the first step to helping someone in need. Although when possible, a living donor is best, it is not for everyone. But ask yourself this, *what are you going to do with your organs once you are deceased?* Each of us has the ability to greatly improve or save a person's life. It is just that simple.

Story Four

Polona Fonda

So what is it like to hate your own body?

Well, it's being disgusted with what you see in the mirror or window reflection, or worst of all, in a photograph. Changing clothes five times in the morning because nothing feels right. Everything seems ugly.

Staying awake all night because another day went bad and ended up with you consuming 10,000 calories. I am not kidding—it's called compulsive overeating.

It's every day trying to wake up without feeling depressed, grasping for that little motivation to just pass another day.

I guess I am just a regular woman with struggles. I've been through no food, lots of food, no food, lots of food again, body hating and having faith in thinking that "skinny" will make me pretty and my life happy.

Well, it didn't! It was even worse, as I ended up obsessed with dieting, compulsive overeating and the painful hate I felt for myself.

As a kid I was a competitive skier, good in sports, always being picked for teams before boys. I was just stronger, so was my body, and that brought comments like:

"Look at those strong legs!"

I still hate that one. Doing sports and wearing shorts became impossible, as everyone, especially men, felt obligated to give me a comment. So the sweet 12 year old turned to eating a carrot a day, trying to get as skinny as possible.

Of course six hours of daily training lead to almost passing out. So at 16, I just quit doing sports, wanting to be a normal teen who does nothing, and looks skinny.

It was too late. I already deeply felt that I was not good enough, which lead to more depressive moods and overeating, stacking on lots of extra kilos. The body hate got even deeper and my vision became "I want to do nothing."

It was a random day and my uncle ran upstairs, screaming to call an ambulance. My grandma had attempted suicide — the one person that every day honestly told me *"You are beautiful"* was giving up.

So was I giving up too? No, I decided to fight.

But little did I know I shouldn't fight, I should love...

I stopped eating, lost 30 kilos, and waited patiently to start feeling happy. It didn't happen.

I started running, went back to fitness, cooking healthy meals, bought tons of makeup and new clothes... nothing helped. Body hate was there, and food being the enemy, stayed there as well. And yet again, where was my confidence?

I knew I had to go back to that little girl that did sports with boys because she loved moving and was proud of being herself and proud of being strong, standing up for her values; instead of trying to stay modest and hide from the world.

Back squats are still my favourite. They were the first exercise I did in my new gym and the comment that accompanied them was, *"You have to use those strong legs you have."* It changed everything.

"So those legs are actually not so bad after all?" Was my thought.

For the first time in my life, I felt a glimpse of being enough, of embracing my body rather than changing it.

There is something about lifting heavy weights that made me feel so powerful. It is about standing back up when something heavy brings you down. It is about learning to be patient. Realizing pain will always be there, but you will learn how to stay calm with it and push through.

Getting to know myself and finding courage to be what I truly am through doing weightlifting and CrossFit — that is my happiness.

It is being a girl that lifts with big quads and wide shoulders, and a woman that is vulnerable but not afraid to feel strong and confident.

Actually training is not about fighting, it is about loving yourself. That's the thin line between injury and health.

Body hate is a real thing. There's no overnight cure, just an everyday decision to try to love yourself. It is like CrossFit — you need consistent training to get stronger.

*****

Polona has recently created a blog for women. If you are interested in following your heart, trusting your intuition, standing up for your values, and making yourself powerful, you will want to visit this blog! http://fondastrong.com/every-woman-lift-heavy-weights/

Story Five

Gordana Jakopcevic

When was the last time you experienced a moment in your life that changed everything?

My story starts when I was 32 years old. Life was pretty typical. I was married, I had three amazing little girls, a great job, a house, and a minivan. I also had this lump in my breast that would periodically come and go.

I went to see doctors who all told me not to worry. They said *"You're young! Women have lumpy breasts. It's totally normal."* They told me to keep up with checkups, continue getting ultrasounds, and not to stress over it. So I followed their advice.

In February of 2008, just to be safe, I went and had a

biopsy. It came back negative! It was such a relief. No cancer.

However, if I'm being honest, aside from my kids, life really wasn't that great. I had a lot going on. I was depressed, I was stressed, I didn't really like my job, and my marriage was breaking down. Worst of all, I didn't like who I was and I really didn't like how I looked or felt. I was hanging on to pregnancy weight. I hid everything in clothes pretty well but I felt uncomfortable in my own skin and I needed change.

I wanted to be happier and healthier.

So I joined a gym. I did the classes, I started spinning and running, and I did minimal weight training. I was so intimidated by the weight room, just like many women are, but I made myself do it anyway. Then a girlfriend of mine told me about this guy who was training out of his garage, doing these crazy workouts, and the results were amazing. She thought it was right up my alley. I went to see him and that's when I was introduced to CrossFit.

This was the first completely life-changing moment. Quickly, working out became my saving grace. I was loving it. However, during that time, that same lump wouldn't go away. In fact, I could feel it more often and at times, I could even see it. It was only the size of a small pea but it was there. And I didn't like it. It had been six months since that biopsy, and I remember thinking, *"I don't care what anyone says, whether it's normal or not, I want it out!* It became a nagging, gut feeling.

Well, you know what they say. Always trust your gut...

In August 2008, I went to the hospital and had a lumpectomy, which is a very minor procedure. I went to the gym in the morning, and the hospital in the afternoon. I was in and out in less than two hours. Awesome, right?

It was gone! I didn't have to think about it any more. Life would go back to normal... Two weeks later, I got the phone call.

This was the second completely life-changing moment.

You can imagine what was running through my head, *"What am I going to do now? I can't have cancer! I'm young, healthy, active! I eat right, I exercise, I follow all the rules, I say please and thank you, I leave 20% tips!"*

So as my life was falling apart — have I mentioned that I was in the middle of a divorce? — I had to accept this news and all that came with it.

I soon learned I would need a mastectomy, followed by chemo, and then more surgery. Out of fear, I postponed my mastectomy three times! **I wasn't afraid of dying**. I was afraid I wouldn't be able to continue this amazing, new lifestyle that I loved!

Would I be able to workout after my surgeries? I couldn't find anyone in my situation. Young and healthy plus CrossFit plus cancer seemed unprecedented. But I decided I wasn't going to let that stop me.

On November 5, 2008, I went to the hospital and they removed my breast. On November 6, I did 100 squats beside my hospital bed.

I was determined to stay fit, to get my range of motion back, and to prove to all of those doctors who told me I wouldn't be able to lift five pounds over my head wrong. And I did. I worked out as much as I could and as often as I could post-surgery and right through six months of chemo.

I blogged about the experience. I wanted a place for women who were in the same situation as me to know that they could do it too. I didn't want another woman to have to search the internet for 'young and healthy plus CrossFit plus cancer' and find nothing.

You can't control everything in life. But you can control what you think and what you do.

There was a point in the beginning, where I wanted to stop being the victim and start writing the story. I needed to hold the reigns.

The more I educated myself about diet and lifestyle

and focusing on my thoughts so that I was silencing the negative chatter that was going on in my head, the better I felt. When I started to learn that things like the quality of your protein sources makes a difference and the benefits of eating plants, about reducing stress and getting enough sleep, it was incredibly liberating.

And then, the most amazing thing happened: I started to feel better.

I moved. I worked out a lot, right through my surgeries and chemo, as much as I could and as often as I could. In my mind, I was building a strong body and a strong immune system. Really, it was more than that. It was emotional and mental as well.

With every workout, I was beating cancer.

I was still not supposed to lift more than 5 to 10 pounds, but when I did, I felt better. I could feel myself getting stronger and it gave me the confidence that I had control over my body.

There were moments when I'd go into chemo sessions — chairs lined with women who had no energy, were weak, and could barely walk — and I'd bounce in, no hair just like them, ready for chemo. One day a woman literally pulled me into the washroom to tell me how amazing I looked and she wanted to so badly know what I was doing. I thought, *"Amazing? We have no eyebrows!"* This was an Aha! moment for me.

It was in this moment that I realized that what I was doing was working and that this new strength that I found wasn't just helping me, it was helping and inspiring other people.

We all have a story. Whether it's cancer or any struggle we've encountered in our lives, we have more power than we think. We don't have to wait for that phone call.

We have power over what we eat, how we move, what we think, the environment we surround ourselves with, and whether we trust and honour our sense of intuition. And even in those life-changing moments, when we are most vulnerable, we can choose strength.

*****

Gordana J. is a coach, writer, and fitness and wellness expert who inspires women to live their healthiest, strongest lives. Learn more and download your free copy of the 5 Best Bodyweight Exercises You Can Do to Get Strong at GordanaJ.com.

Story Six

Daniel Crane

"And the day came when the risk to remain tight in a bud was more painful than the risk it took to blossom."
~ Anais Nin

On the evening of July 28, 2012, my future was ripe with potential. I was in the prime of my life, serving my country in the United States Air Force. I was stationed in paradise, following in the footsteps of my father and hell-bent on making a difference and saving lives.

That night though...my life was the one that needed saving.

It was around midnight when I walked to my car, the

hot, humid island air interrupted by a salty breeze. I put my key into the ignition, my thoughts still reveling in a night spent with friends and laughter.

In my periphery, a vehicle pulled alongside my passenger window and the hairs of my neck stood on end. Instantaneously, I saw a flash, slowly followed by the loud "bang" of a slug shot from a shotgun at point-blank range. The anti-military individual sped away as quickly as he arrived, leaving me in a sweaty, stifling haze, the sulfurous smell of the gunshot dangling in the air.

As I struggled to assess the damage and regain my composure, I felt a warm, wet sensation on my arm. Looking down, blood poured through my fingers, accompanying what I later would learn were a destroyed bicep, mangled nerves, damaged blood vessels, and a severed brachial artery.

All I knew was that I was losing blood quickly and needed help.

Adrenaline took over, and I exited the car, running only about 25 meters before dropping to my knees. Unable to open the gate latch to my friend's house, I mustered what I thought were my last few words and cried for help as I struggled to survive. Miraculously, my friend found me and called for help. I was stabilized and then medically evacuated from Guam.

Grateful to be alive, the real work began. Eight

surgeries and several attempts to regenerate nerves from my arm, I finally elected to amputate. The decision came with a mixed bag of emotions — relief from the stress of additional surgeries, finality, and a realization that I was likely closing a door to military service. I didn't go down without a fight, but I hoped that if this door closed, it would open a window.

It did.

I haven't looked back, nor have I slowed down. Physical therapy was grueling. I needed to relearn everything on my other hand. I had to reinvent myself.

What did my life have in store for me? I didn't have to look far.

I took to Archery like a fish to water, learning how to shoot a bow with one arm and a mouth tab. I became a formidable threat to my sister services as part of both the Warrior Games and Invictus Games, Olympic-style events for wounded warriors.

In 2014, I was honored to participate, at the request of His Royal Highness, Prince Harry of Wales, in an archery demonstration by those athletes, competing using mouth tabs rather than their arms, and I was awarded the Inspirational Award by the Prince himself.

Sport was the turning point in the reinvention of myself. I realized that sport was so much greater than myself. I learned the value of teamwork, and as wounded warriors, we work together to win, but we also help each other move forward in life.

This journey was no longer mine alone. When I won the Inspiration Award at the Invictus Games in London, I learned that sportsmanship can inspire just by going out there and competing. I realized the magnitude of what I was doing — no excuses, just go out and be awesome.

Along the journey of sport, I discovered CrossFit and appreciated its intensity, as well as its physical and mental challenges. It has been one of the few constants in my life — something that I did before the attack.

Stepping into my new normal, I was still able to take a few valuable things with me, and CrossFit was one of my few mainstays and a bedrock of my physical well-being.

With one arm, as with any injury, I had to find safe and creative workarounds. I mastered single arm power cleans. I used a prosthetic for pull-ups and kettlebells. I stumbled. I laughed. Sometimes, I impressed the ladies. And as in my other sports experiences, I found kinship and camaraderie in like-minded people.

There is a lot of therapy in just doing the work. I pushed further, getting my CrossFit Level-1 and

CrossFit Mobility Trainer certifications. And then that window was opened for me.

Today, I recognize that my military service will always be a part of who I am. So will my injury. So will CrossFit. But none will define me.

As I make the transition to coach and trainer, I hope to specifically find others who walk in the same shoes that I once did as they try to establish a new normal. My hope is that I save more lives in the gym than I ever could on the battlefield through the love of sport and sweat.

No excuses. Just be awesome.

Story Seven

Philippa Roy

I remember the day my body changed like it was yesterday...

However, in actual fact it was seven years ago now that I got up to walk to the front door of the hairdressing salon where I was employed and my left leg didn't seem to work properly. It got progressively worse over the following few months, and people started to notice that I was limping.

I was firmly in denial but finally, I phoned my mum in tears because I felt so sure that I had the disease that had been passed down to me through my dad, and through his dad before him. Sure enough, the DNA tests came back positive: I was diagnosed with something called Spinocerebellar Ataxia Type 3

(SCA3), otherwise known as Machado-Joseph Disease.

SCA3 is a hereditary, degenerative condition which has been traced back to the Azores in Portugal, and two families in particular, from which the disease gets its name. There is no known cure.

It affects the part of the brain that controls movement. By the time I was diagnosed I was 36. My dad had died at the age of 61 and I remember thinking that I had to make the most of every day that I had. To do that I needed to make some changes to my life and while I was frightened of what the future held for me, I found an inner strength from somewhere and decided that nothing was going to stop me from achieving my goals.

My first goal was to work for myself and go freelance. By that time I had built up a loyal and sizable clientele. This gave me the flexibility I needed to go for my second goal, which was more about my health and really coming to grips with managing my condition effectively.

You see, there is no medicine for my condition. There are drugs that can just about manage the worst of the symptoms, and I take drugs for people with Parkinson's Disease. This meant that I had to give up alcohol and develop a more nutritious diet. It was pretty tough, but I soon got used to that, and also to leading a much quieter lifestyle than I had been living to that point!

The biggest breakthrough for me, however (apart from meeting my future husband, Michael, in 2011), was when I discovered CrossFit later that year.

CrossFit was unlike anything I had ever done before. Not that I was ever very sporty. I have never really stuck at any kind of exercise before — or any kind of "club" for that matter (apart from nightclubs!) — but it involved such a range of different exercises, all focusing on different areas such as strength, endurance, balance and mobility, that I never felt bored. Plus, it seemed to be exactly what my body needed and it responded almost immediately.

For example, before CrossFit, when I was at my lowest, I remember feeling scared to go out of the house to go shopping, simply because I couldn't balance properly. I would shake and sway and often fall over.

I avoided meeting people because I was embarrassed about the way I walked. People would stare at me in the street as if I was drunk, or they were concerned that I had hurt myself. But CrossFit changed all that.

My balance got better almost overnight. My walking gait improved and I wasn't tripping over so much. As I worked harder and harder, I got more and more toned. I had muscles for the first time! People started to notice my new physique. The confidence this gave me encouraged me to make new friends and renew old relationships.

One thing that everyone notices about a good CrossFit box is the feeling of community. Everyone at CrossFit Glasgow, and in the wider CrossFit community, around the city and beyond, have been supportive and encouraging, right from the very beginning.

Certain exercises are always going to be really challenging for me, particularly those that involve balance, but I'm improving all the time and when I think back to what I was like before, it's like the difference between night and day.

Near the beginning of my training, for example, jumping for me was simply out of the question. I mean, not at all: I couldn't even jump an inch. I remember the day that I first attempted to jump on a 5 kg plate. I had to hold my trainer's hands. But eventually, after a few false starts, I did it. I remember such a tremendous feeling of accomplishment at what now seems such a small thing. But by the beginning of the CrossFit Open in 2012, I was able to jump — unaided — on a 20 inch box. And not just once, but 15 times! And not only jump: I am now able to do burpees, skip, bench press, push press, deadlift, and strict pull-ups, and I'm now progressing towards strict muscle-ups and even handstands.

I can't believe that I'm actually competing. My trainers at CrossFit Glasgow encourage me to compete in the

Open, and I have every year for the last three.

I have also had the opportunity to share my story with the Spirit of the Games, with a view to helping and encouraging others who might have a similar story to tell. I think that this was probably the spur for me to get involved in a number of different groups, particularly in relation to adaptive athletes in CrossFit, but also local support groups for those with Ataxia. This is something I hope to get more involved in. I also aim to attain the Level 1 CrossFit Certification course in the near future, and maybe help out with training.

I vividly remember being in denial about my condition before. I'm no longer in denial, but I can honestly say that most of the time I hardly even think about it. That's down to the fact that, in all likelihood, nobody meeting me for the first time would ever know that I have a condition.

In fact, my neurologist can't believe the difference in me and the progress that I have made in the last few years. All of the tests indicate that I'm back to within normal ranges; in other words, ranges for someone without a degenerative neurological condition.

I can honestly say that CrossFit has changed my life.

Of course, I look forward to the day that a cure is announced for my condition. A group of scientists in

Portugal are said to be close. I have decided never to have children, in case it is passed on to them, but I live a full life anyway. No matter what the future holds for me, I don't think anyone can ever accuse me of not living my life to the fullest.

*****

Philippa Roy is now currently maintaining her fitness, while getting involved in motivational speaking. She has a Facebook page called Sink or Swim, which she updates regularly.

Story Eight

Sara Michelle Vis

At 18 years old I was 5 foot 6, 89 pounds and diagnosed with Anorexia Nervosa. My life and future were decaying before me just as rapidly as my health. This was three years ago.

From a young age I was very active, playing hockey, soccer, volleyball, track, dance...you name it. I used to pride myself on my big powerful legs and my bulking muscles because I was strong, physically and mentally.

The summer before grade 12, I decided that I was going to start making healthier choices in the kitchen so that I could be a better version of me. Unfortunately, as many may know, I am a total type-A personality and have to do everything 100%.

Throughout the summer, I lost a little weight, nothing significant, but attributed it mostly to losing my "hockey bulk." During the school year I stopped playing hockey and devoted my time to dance, racking up more than 20 hours a week in the studio.

By mid-year I weighed 105 pounds and I thought I looked great, and I was doing all of the "healthy" things that were all over the media. However, since I was losing weight quickly, my parents thought it would be beneficial to start working with a nutritionist to ensure that my caloric intake matched my energy output.

At the end of the year I was sitting at 100 pounds and had many teachers, friends and family expressing their concern. My thoughts? *"They're crazy, I'm totally fine!"* Who cares if I don't have any energy? It's just because I'm dancing so much.

The summer after graduation, my health took a turn for the worst.

I became obsessed with everything I was putting in my body. It was like a game: How could I make the lowest calorie meal possible while still feeling full? I used to leave my friends to go home and cook my meals because God forbid, anyone else have control over my food. As a result of this, nearing the end of the summer, I was lonely and wasting away at 89 pounds, eating less than 700 calories a day.

I will never forget the day I call "The Ultimate Collapse": A spontaneous plan to go out for dinner with my boyfriend, Andrew, and a friend, left me in a full blown panic attack, shaking uncontrollably.

I remember seeing such fear in my boyfriend's eyes. How was I supposed to control anything at the restaurant? What if they put oil in my food? After calming myself down, I remember thinking *"Why am I like this? What have I turned into?"* I knew I needed help.

At the end of the summer, my mom took me to see an eating disorder specialist. She told me that if I weren't 18 years old I would have been removed from every aspect of my life and forced into an institution, that my heart rate and blood pressure were so low that if I kept it up for another year, I had a high chance of fatal organ failure.

Here's a peek inside my head: At this point, threats to my life weren't enough to motivate me to change my delusional view of my health because I was the smallest I'd ever been. I was exactly what society wanted me to be.

Makes sense, right?

Didn't think so. Minds of those with eating disorders are distorted and irrational, and the worst part is that it isn't something you can just "snap out of."

The doctor started me on a 2800-calorie diet, adding 200 calories at each weekly appointment until I hit 4000. I would cry while eating due to physical pain and self-disgust. I was forced to quit dance. My life was miserable. But I didn't see it as a choice any more. I knew if I wanted my life back I just had to do it, whether I wanted to or not.

I couldn't have done any of that if it wasn't for my parents, both of whom played two very different roles for me. My mom was the one who had to use tough-love, the one I yelled at and took out my frustration and pain on; she took it day in and day out and I thank her eternally for that.

My dad was the reassurance when I felt like I couldn't take another second, the one who, with a single look, knew when I didn't want to talk any more and just needed a hug.

Though times were tough, I got through the year and by the following summer I was back up to 108 pounds. I stopped seeing my doctors, and I was mentally doing okay.

I went away for school in the fall but things got bad again quickly; by Christmas I was back to 95 pounds and was controlling my food intake. The difference this time was that I recognized the sick, ghostly girl that I was. My parents threatened not to let me go back, but I told them I could do it, that I could fix myself for good.

About a month later I started meeting with my mentor, Richard. This man saved me; he made me want to fight to get better. His enthusiasm was genuine and he set me up with a nutrition and training program with research articles explaining why he had me eating the way I was, proof that what I was doing was beneficial.

About two weeks in, I was shown *The Paleo Solutions* podcast and as I listened, it all sounded very familiar... I was unaware at the time, but Rich had actually started me on a 90%-compliant high fat, high protein, and moderate carb athlete's Paleo diet.

Within a few days I decided to take out the gluten, grains and dairy, add more organics, grass-fed beef, omega-3 eggs and fish oil, and dive in head first. I started crushing my workouts, making great progress, and I was so full of life and energy, a feeling I hadn't felt in far too long.

I was happy for the first time in two years.

Several months later, early December of 2014, I discovered CrossFit. I started by trying a few movements on my own, watching videos and testing it out. Then upon coming home for Christmas break, I walked into Undefeated CrossFit and instantly fell in love: the people, the challenge, everything. I had finally found my niche. **This is who I am.**

During my short time home, I developed a really great relationship with my coach and owner of Undefeated. Matt offered to program for me while I was back at school. After dancing for 17 years, the gymnastic and bodyweight movements were a breeze for me, conquering butterfly pull-ups and handstand walks in my first three months.

It is the brute-strength component that sets a pretty big limit; yes, you could say I am "strong for my size," but I want more, I crave more. I'm that girl who, if you tell her she can't do something, she is going to do absolutely everything in her power to do it. With CrossFit, when I see I'm not strong enough to do a workout Rx, next time I'm in the gym I'm going to do everything I can to gain the strength I need to not be limited in that workout again.

Matt has encouraged me in every step along the way, showing such enthusiasm for my potential. He once told me, *"There are ones who were born athletic and ones we try to make athletic. You're the first kind. A natural who just 'gets it' and it's really up to the coach to take them as far as they can."*

While my restrictions keep me pushing towards my goals, they have also taught me patience, to not be so hard on myself and to celebrate all victories, no matter how small. This point has really been reinforced by the CrossFit community, like when I post things on my Instagram and get awesome comments from people I have never met, or my friends giving me a boost when I'm having an off day.

Matt has also challenged me in so many ways, physically and mentally, and I have learned a lot about myself thanks to him — what I am capable of, learning how to be confident in my abilities, and how much more I have to offer the world than I ever thought I did.

I lost a lot of friends through the journey of sickness and recovery, and the relationship I have with my coach, along with all of the encouragement and support I have from my parents, reminds me that someone wants me to be a better version of myself too, that someone else thinks I'm capable of it and is supporting me through every obstacle and accomplishment.

This was the last hurdle for me in overcoming my disorder. This showed me that life is much greater than the size of clothing I wear, that my body is powerful and beautiful and that I won't treat it as anything less.

Every day I step into the gym to train, I am filled with happiness and I am excited to get one step closer to being a better me. Yes, there are days when I'm sore and would rather sleep past 5:30 am, but I remember the months when happiness was an unattainable goal, a feeling so foreign and distorted.

Joy is something that a lot of people take for granted, something most think is just there; it's bittersweet, but I believe that you never really know how special true happiness is until it is taken away from you.

You're responsible for creating your own happiness, surrounding yourself with people and an environment that helps you thrive.

I am one of the lucky ones; people battle this disorder their entire life. While a lot of it came from the little fire that burned inside of me to keep going, growing bigger and bigger as I overcame each obstacle, the reason I am here today is because of the people that I am so blessed to have had support me.

Andrew, Richard, my few friends who stayed by my side, my dance teachers Rob and Lori, my brothers Matthew and Daniel, Matt, and most importantly my parents. I owe you all my life... literally, and I thank you for that.

*****

Sara is currently studying at the University of Western Ontario, pursuing a career in the health and medical community with the intent of sharing her story, knowledge, and passion to better the lives of others. See what she is up to by following her Instagram account @_saravis

Story Nine

David Chesworth

Ever since I can remember, I have always wanted to know the feeling of being able to do a standing back tuck. The idea of being completely suspended in the air while maintaining full body control was fascinating to me.

For an everyday gymnast, this is a basic movement. But for me, the thought of this gave me the same feeling I get when I look up at the night sky and wonder what the universe is like up there.

I wanted to explore the fitness universe. And I wanted to start by doing a standing back tuck. But I was always too afraid. I did not believe it to be possible within me. It was not until I found my passion for CrossFit that I discovered a self dominance I never knew possible. I finally felt ready to begin a progression for the standing back tuck.

It was a day like any other. It was my third week going to a gymnastics gym to supplement my CrossFit training. Not only that, but I was also working up towards a standing back tuck. It was the very end of a workout and I had felt a sense of mastery of the back tuck on the bouncy tumble track.

The gym was closing for the night, which meant the tumble track needed to be deflated and packed up. The owner of the gym suggested I continue practicing skills on the floor while they cleaned up. With mixed feelings, I approached the mat, wondering if attempting a standing back tuck would be a good idea. I felt ready for it, and yet, I was tired and not completely sure of myself.

The coach on staff wanted me to be more confident so she pepped me up with a lot of positive reinforcement. She asked if I needed a spot. I asked her what she thought would be best. She said she believed in me, so go for it.

I cleared my mind of all thoughts, took a deep breath, and jumped. Although it was a sloppy landing, I had just successfully landed my very first ever standing back tuck. I was doing it. I was experiencing the fitness universe. Not only that, it was my very first try.

Wanting to perform better, I attempted again.

This time, I slightly under-rotated and landed on all fours. Frustrated, I got up and tried again. This time, landing on my shoulder. Being tired, and it being a high skill activity, I decided to just give it one more go and then call it a day afterwards, no matter what.

I took a deep breath, cleared my thoughts, and jumped. In this moment, life became slow motion, as I knew I had completely under-rotated... BAM! I had just landed on the back of my neck. In less than a second, the course of my life instantly changed as I had just received three fractures in my C1 and C2 vertebrae. These vertebrae surround the part of the spinal cord that control breathing and heart beat. Upon taking the x-rays the doctors told me, *"Don't move, this is life or death, don't move."*

Not only was my body in shock from the injury, but my mind was also in shock from the news that at any given moment, or the slightest wrong movement, everything could be over...everything.

At that moment, everything that truly mattered to me came rushing through my mind. *"What if I never see my family again? What if I never have a family of my own? What if I never see my friends again? What if I never move again?"*

The look on the neurosurgeon's face, while always positive and calming as he needed to be, was still giving off a sense of fear and uncertainty about the outcome of my situation. The fractures, being one millimeter away from my spinal cord, left him with a difficult decision.

Should he carefully adjust my head and a attach a Halo brace for a natural bone fusion, or should he go in and fuse my cervical vertebrae together? If he fused my vertebrae, I would never again be able to shake my head, yes or no.

Fortunately for me, he decided it was worth it to attempt the Halo procedure.

Also fortunately for me, the procedure was successful.

For two months my mom moved into my apartment with me. While I was depressed to have lost my independence, during these two months my eyes were opened with many realizations.

People I hadn't spoken to since elementary school reached out to me. People cared about me. Not only that, I impacted these people and didn't even know it.

Many of the first people to pay me a visit in the hospital were friends I made at CrossFit Hilton Head/ Conviction Training Facility. I also began to understand just how important it is to allow myself to accept help from others when I need it. I didn't have to do this alone.

How fortunate was I to have had such an incredible bonding experience with my mother as a young adult like this. Not too many young guys out of college can say that. How fortunate was I to have learned what it truly means to be patient. The rest of my body felt ready to go at all times, but was halted by the vulnerability of my neck.

The human being is only as ready as its least ready component...

Maybe I couldn't do much, but I was forced to stop focusing on what I couldn't do, and to start focusing on what I COULD do! I could walk! You better believe I walked. My mom and I signed up for a 5k on the beach together. We walked the whole thing side by side. We were the last to cross the finish line, but we couldn't have felt more like first place winners.

One of the most motivational aspects of my recovery was my CrossFit Gym. Soon after my injury, the CrossFit Open began. Every Saturday morning at 9 am, for five weeks, everyone at the gym came together to complete the CrossFit Open workouts. Everyone came together as one team, not just to compete but to live a healthier, more active life together.

I remember feeling so bummed that I was unable to participate, but my mom and I were there every week to watch everyone workout. I was amazed at how many people came up to me to tell me how inspired they were to have me there, and that they would push harder simply because they saw me on the sidelines. Not only that, but to see them competing in the Open gave me another thing to look forward to. I could envision myself in their shoes as a healed man competing in the Open workouts one day. This became just one more reason that I had to recover to the best of my ability so that I could have a chance at competing in a future Open competition.

During my time in the Halo, one of my friends from CTF, Anne, suggested that I blog my recovery as inspiration to others as they follow my journey. I thought, *"What a great idea!"* This was a great way to put more positivity into an overall negative situation.

I decided to log my journey in the form of motivational videos. Not only was this therapeutic for me, but I hoped that by doing this I could inspire others out there to never give up. Especially when things get tough, and especially when things feel out of your control. I hope to show others that the human body is an unbelievable thing. It is one of the few things in life that will always be there for you. The human body is a precious thing and it should be taken care of in the form of a healthy lifestyle.

10 months after my injury, I had my final x-ray. I had done everything the doctor told me to do. With the

feeling of my life constantly on the line, I did not want to mess this up. When my neurosurgeon showed me my x-ray, he looked me in the eyes and said, *"You are 100% healed. With the exception of some scar tissue, it looks as if nothing ever happened."* He said, *"David, you are free of limitations."*

Today, I am back at the CrossFit gym continuing my exploration of the Fitness Universe. Although it may not have been pretty, I can honestly say that I have successfully done one standing back tuck. Check! Acrobatics are off the list; on to the next adventure.

Upon returning to the gym, I approached my head coach, Craig, with my vision of being a fitness astronaut. I told him that my next mission is to be a part of the 1000 pound club. This is when your 1RM bench press, back squat, and deadlift add up to 1000 or more pounds.

Craig jumped all over this and helped me design a program that is safe and effective for my return to exercise. We both agreed that the number one priority with this goal, as it should be with anything, is form and safety. Only once I have reached a certain level of form mastery will we think about moving up in weight.

Whether it be during a group training or open gym, people from my CrossFit community are always there cheering me on, cueing me with helpful tips on good form and, most importantly, asking me how I am. It's the little things like this that go a long way!

The feeling of walking into a gym and knowing that I am cared about gives me a feeling that I can do anything.

With this combination of confidence that I have acquired from CrossFit and the patience and wisdom I've gained from my recovery, I truly do believe that I can do anything I set my mind to. If I can dream it, I can live it.

When I started my 1000 pound club journey half a year ago, my total was 695 pounds. I have been going to CTF a minimum of three times per week and am now up to an 890 pounds total. Before I know it, I may have to up the ante on my goal!

The human body is an unbelievable thing. I am proud to be one of countless examples of this as I continue on my journey. And maybe, just maybe, I will meet, inspire, and be inspired by more people along the way.

On one final note, I am proud to say that I was recovered enough to participate in the CrossFit Open workouts this year (2015). Everyone at the gym was so excited to have me back that I was asked to be a team captain for our workouts! The words, "I CAN," that CrossFit preaches, take you a long way.

Last year I was physically unable to workout, period.

Here I am, one year later as a team captain for a competition of very challenging workouts. I may not have won any of the workouts, but I did them. And I did them injury free and felt like a true winner.

*****

David is a Fitness Coach at Hilton Head Health, Weight Loss and Wellness Resort. He leads through example by continually seeking to become a better version of himself through living a healthy lifestyle.

Story Ten

Anonymous

I was always an athlete, starting from a young age. I played a wide variety of competitive sports with most of my focus and efforts spent on gymnastics, golf and racing downhill (skiing). Athletics came naturally to me. I was always a good athlete in the sports I played throughout school but never a great one.

I did have pressure, albeit not intentional, to be great at the sports I played. I was always encouraged to practice more, to eliminate weaknesses, to not be afraid, to refine movements — always having something scrutinized and critiqued yet also never in an overbearing way.

I never wanted to disappoint anyone in telling them that what they wanted for me wasn't what I wanted for me, that I was okay being good and didn't need to be great.

Over the years, as I grew up, much of this added up to me building a view of myself that I was not "good enough" and I started to carry this throughout my life in general.

During those formidable high school years, carrying around the feeling of not being good enough was further perpetuated by not "fitting in" with any particular crowd. I wasn't 'not' part of a crowd, but never truly part of one either. I just "was." Now that I'm older, I'm actually thankful that I wasn't part of a labelled crowd during those years but, at that time, it did add to the sense of not being good enough to fully belong.

Fast forward to my final year of high school, which was largely full of normal and unremarkable teenage experiences, except that I was sexually assaulted and told nobody about it.

I grew up in a small town where word spreads like wildfire. As a teenager who already doubted her self worth, this was one of the last things I wanted attention being drawn to. I convinced myself that the stories that would spread or the lies that would be told would far outweighed any good that would come from reporting it. Never mind what was going through my mind as to what my father would do if he knew.

So I buried it in the back of my mind and lived with it and the repeated questions in my head that I couldn't ignore about why it happened, what I did to deserve it or, worse, to "ask for it."

I prayed that I wouldn't run into the person any time that I left the house.

Time went by and I had my escape when I moved out

of town to go to post-secondary school. I would go home for the summers, but those months away at school helped me to try and forget.

Out of sight, out of mind...

I was home for one summer and it happened again. I was sexually assaulted by two people at a friend's party. The shame, guilt, agony, blame and humiliation started all over again. Once again, I chose to not say a word to anyone for the same reasons as before and waited it out until I could go back to school — trying to ignore it again.

By the time I hit adulthood I had developed a very poor sense of self-worth and very low self-esteem. If someone paid me a compliment, if someone took interest in me, if someone thought I did something well — I was always skeptical of their intentions, wondering what they wanted because I wasn't the kind of person who was deserving of their praise or attention. I couldn't be, I thought, I wasn't good enough for that. This lead to a number of unhealthy relationships as life went along.

I had a failed marriage in my early twenties. Looking back, not only was I too young to have gotten married, but it was to a person who lowered my self-esteem even further to a point where, at 25 years old, I was convinced that nobody would ever want me if I left, and that, at 105 pounds (5'3"), I was fat and unattractive.

I was depressed and I had developed a very unhealthy relationship with food. Alcohol became an escape for me too.

I had a couple of friendships I had developed through work that were instrumental in convincing me to leave (my marriage) for my own sake and helped me make a new start and work on rebuilding myself.

A number of years later, following much effort to repair my self-esteem, I married a wonderful man whom I had been with for four years.

Unfortunately, that wonderful man turned out to be not so wonderful after we got married and I was a passenger in a four year emotional train wreck. After battling to hang on and finding that I was using alcohol to escape my life again, I made the decision to take care of myself and left my second marriage.

Now I held the view of being a failure on top of still carrying a deeply rooted "not good enough" view of myself. The failed marriage was followed by another longer-term relationship which was a slow drip of verbal abuse that often included daily use of the word "stupid" in reference to my interests, thoughts or feelings. It was during this last, unhealthy relationship that I discovered CrossFit.

From the first time I tried CrossFit, it gave me a sense

of purpose. It was so different from anything I'd ever done. The environment I walked into was welcoming and encouraging, and they didn't even know me.

I did one class and was hooked on the challenge and, after a few months, the competitive aspect awoke the former athlete in me — a much stronger and more determined one than I'd ever known.

Instead of scrutiny and pressure, I received support and encouragement. I was also part of an eclectic group of people where I felt like I belonged. I didn't have to be someone I wasn't, and nobody considered me stupid. It was okay to screw up, make a mistake, fail.

Failure was encouraged because it was a key part of developing and learning. Not once was I ever told, nor did I feel, that I wasn't good enough. Not once did I ever hear anyone spoken to as though they weren't good enough, no matter their level of ability or fitness. The support of others and the friendships I was building helped to strengthen my character. It gave me the strength to start standing up for myself and push back on things that didn't make me happy, which included people in my life who were not good for me.

Soon, the bad relationships dissolved and other, more important meaningful ones flourished.

For six years, CrossFit has continued to challenge me while being fun at the same time. I don't think I've ever seriously stuck with anything for so long! The variety of movements to work on and master has been able to capture and hold my attention.

CrossFit is always something different every day; it is always interesting. I am also good at it, really good. I have areas that definitely need a lot of work, but it was the first thing I found that I was really good at and others saw the potential for me to be great without turning me off of it.

This wonderfully supportive environment was instrumental in helping me achieve a dream I had set for myself in 2012 — to qualify for the CrossFit Games. I put in the hard work and countless hours training. With my CrossFit friends by my side encouraging me, I realized my dream with a trip to the CrossFit Games in 2014.

Most importantly, my CrossFit family is what keeps me going back and is what has helped shaped me as a coach who wants nothing more than to see others improve and make a difference in their own lives.. At 36, I finally found my athletic calling and a place where I belonged among a community of incredibly supportive people — all of whom started out as strangers, many of whom have become close friends.

CrossFit has enabled me to become a stronger person both physically and, more importantly, mentally. CrossFit has helped me to overcome some very bad body image issues and provided me with the means to develop healthy relationships with food. I now have the closest relationships with friends that I've ever been capable of having and have more confidence in myself than I have ever had in my life.

Story Eleven

Julie Hartman

What started as a small gathering place for a few friends who were looking for something to do during volleyball offseason, has become a powerful and fierce community of strong women, most of whom would never had crossed paths if it weren't for "the garage."

The original intent of the garage was simply to be a place I could workout after having my second child and no longer had the time to make it to our local CrossFit affiliate.

Next, it was a weekly Saturday workout with friends and family where I shared my hobby. Before we knew it, the 'Big Mommas' were born.

My husband and I began gathering equipment (bought, borrowed, dragged out of basements and sheds), and in less than six months we had a fully functioning CrossFit garage gym on our hands.

Living in a small town, news traveled fast. Without any advertising or encouraging, there was a group of 15-20 women showing up for classes, three times per week. This is where the magic began.

The garage soon became a sanctuary for our members, a place to be yourself — unapologetically. The community that so quickly formed provided us with a safe space to be vulnerable as we tackled our CrossFit goals.

The functional element of CrossFit training so easily translates into the lives of the 'Big Mommas.' We farmer carry our six bags of groceries into the house, just so we can proudly admit we did it all in one trip. We push press our toddlers in the air when we play. We can deadlift heavy furniture when helping a friend move into her new house.

We make it through horrendous work days by silently repeating in our heads *"this isn't as bad as a hill sprint...this isn't as bad as a hill sprint."*

We are confident and stand up for ourselves because we are used to dealing with scary people like Fran, Cindy, and Grace. We've learned that, as a group, there isn't much we aren't capable of.

CrossFit provides a training program that delivers

unarguable physical changes. The 'Big Mommas' are stronger, faster and more powerful than when we started.

These physiological changes do not occur without affecting our minds and spirits. We've become more confident and less judgmental, more kind and less concerned with others' opinions. More knowledgeable and less worried. More focused and less ashamed.

We have overcome a battle that so many females struggle with for a lifetime: We are not ashamed of our bodies; we do not apologize for what we can do; we are driven to improve and burst with pride when we reach a goal; and our body is our vehicle to get the job done, so damn right we love it!

Sure, any old group of gals that get together can create a sense of community. But what sets CrossFit apart from the running groups, bridge clubs, and scrapbookers of the world is that it provides a platform upon which women can do something they have typically been told not to do: be loud and strong.

In my humble opinion (not so humble maybe), nothing is more fiercely unstoppable than a group of strong, beautiful, confident women who don't give a sh*t what others have to say about them!

Story Twelve

Anna Hartman

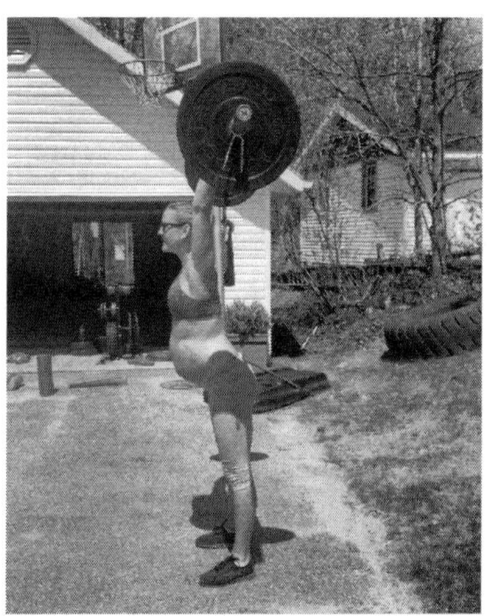

In the fall of 2012, I started to notice that my morning walks with my dog Larry were not as energizing as they used to be. I would take Larry to the waterfront near my home each morning so he could run off some energy and I could clear my head for the busy day ahead of me.

Growing up, I had always been an athlete and was currently training for my first half-marathon later that fall and attending CrossFit classes two to three times per week. Despite being in great shape, I would get short of breath on these morning walks and felt light headed. I would return home to grab breakfast and head off to work. By the time I arrived at work, I would feel a little better and get on with my day.

I didn't think too much about my "feeling off" until I realised I hadn't felt like my regular, energetic self for over a month. Along with the weakness in the mornings, I had started to drink a lot of water. I was constantly thirsty and riding a roller coaster of feeling faint to feeling very lethargic.

I finally decided to call my family doctor to book an appointment.

When I was speaking with the nurse on the phone about my list of symptoms, she asked me to wait a moment as she wanted to speak to my doctor. With her hand over the speaker I heard her whisper *"I think Anna Hartman is diabetic."*

It only took one simple blood test to show that at the age of 27, my pancreas had stopped creating insulin, and I was a Type 1 Diabetic. There are few moments in life that stop you in your tracks like this one did for me.

I had always taken care of my body through healthy eating and exercise and it didn't seem possible that I was a diabetic. Overnight, I was forced to learn how to count carbs and administer four shots of insulin daily.

The reality of my diagnosis quickly set in. I wondered

if my fast paced, active lifestyle was a reality for me any more. My main concern was whether my illness would prevent me from having a healthy baby. My main goal became getting my sugars within a range that I could get pregnant and carry a healthy baby full-term.

Leading up to my diagnosis, CrossFit classes had become an important part of my life. I was lucky enough to be a part of a garage gym full of my friends and instructed by my sister; we liked to call ourselves the 'Big Mommas.'

Nearly 20 of us would get together three times a week and throw down a WOD in my sister's garage. We all support one another as we each go through life's ups and downs and I knew that I needed the "garage" to help me through this huge transition. I would monitor my sugars closely and listened to my body as I slowly got back to RX'ing a WOD with the huge support of my 'Big Mommas.'

Within five months, I was able to manage my diabetes and had my sugars in a healthy range, and within a year I was pregnant!

Now it was back to my 'Big Mommas' to help me through my next big challenge. My sister offered me great modifications as I continued through each trimester and I was able to stay active and keep my sugars in a healthy range throughout my entire pregnancy.

My beautiful baby boy was born on July 1, 2014, and after six weeks off to recover from a C-section, I was back at the garage.

From the beginning, I made a conscious decision that diabetes would not limit my lifestyle. I would learn to do all the things I love to do and be diabetic. Three years ago, I was a healthy woman that loved to CrossFit; today, I am a healthy CrossFit Mom, who just happens to have diabetes.

Story Thirteen

Danielle Smith

All I wanted was for this pain to go away. My anxious mind was in constant worry; all my thoughts were overwhelming and destructive, spiraling me into a depressive state. My chest was tight, my stomach in knots, I couldn't eat, I would cry uncontrollably for hours and hours worrying about never being able to escape my thoughts and get out of this dark place that my mind had entered.

Every day tasks seemed unbearable; work and relationships were unmanageable. Sleep did not come easy. I was sad all the time. Although I knew I would never act on it, thoughts of suicide entered my mind. I wished for something bad to happen to me in order to mask the internal pain I was feeling. I thought people would sympathize more if my pain were physical.

I felt alone and disconnected from reality. My motivation and energy were non-existent, I was utterly exhausted: emotionally, physically, and mentally.

Life felt like such a struggle.

This wasn't me. I am a strong, confident and intelligent woman; why couldn't I stop feeling this way? I knew I needed help. I made an appointment with my family physician and he diagnosed me with General Anxiety Disorder and depression.

After that appointment, my road to recovery began. I saw my family physician regularly, was referred to a psychiatrist, spoke to a psychotherapist, and have had numerous counseling sessions with a social worker. It has been quite the journey, which I am still currently traveling, and it has definitely had its obstacles.

I suffered with episodes of anxiety attacks, which contributed to some social anxiety as I feared experiencing an attack in front of people. I was extremely sensitive to medications; some made me feel even worse. I thought the pain I was experiencing was never going to end and all I wanted was to be my strong, confident, and vibrant self again.

The one aspect of my life that I was able to keep constant was 'Big Momma's House of Pain,' our CrossFit garage. No matter how bad of a day I was having or how much I did not want to get out of bed, I forced myself to attend 'Big Momma's' and do a WOD.

The garage is not just a space to do CrossFit; 'Big Momma's' is an inclusive and non-judgmental place where women can come together and be physically active. The sport of CrossFit and 'Big Momma's' has been essential in getting myself healthy again.

When I am at my worst, I still manage to get to the garage. Although I am exhausted and feel the weakest I have ever been, for the hour I am there, I am strong.

I am beyond grateful to have the support system of 'Big Momma's.' I am not sure where I would be without the escape of CrossFit at the garage. I have done things there I never thought I could accomplish: pull-ups, double-unders, handstand push-ups along with fighting a mental illness.

All completed with the support of a great group of women who are strong, confident, beautiful, healthy, and fit.

As I continue my journey in coping with General Anxiety Disorder and depression, I decided to have an affirmation for myself that I could refer to for encouragement and support during my bad times or days I wasn't at the garage surrounded by all the 'Big Momma's.'

My Affirmation – I am Strong...

I am strong mentally.

I am strong because I am brave.

I am strong because I have friends and family who love and support me.

I am strong physically.

I am strong because I love myself.

I am strong because I am not ashamed of my illness.

I am strong emotionally.

I am strong because I won't let GAD define me.

I am strong because I am hopeful.

I am strong because I am not afraid to seek help.

I am strong because I am proud of who I am.

I am strong socially.

I am strong because I am a fighter.

I am strong because I want to be better.

I am strong because I will persevere.

I am strong because I am confident in myself.

I am strong because I know my weaknesses.

I am strong because I will share my story.

I am strong because I can be honest with others and myself.

I am strong because I have BIG MOMMA'S!

Story Fourteen

Aimee Piech

My love for CrossFit came unexpectedly, but at the perfect time in my life. Prior to CrossFit, I had been involved in physical activity throughout high school (rowing, basketball and volleyball) and really enjoyed being connected to each of them.

I had always considered myself to be a fairly strong athlete and in pretty good shape overall. At the age of 25, I met my perfect match, Ken. From the moment I connected with him, I had a pretty strong feeling that he was the one I would marry. He was kind, loyal, honest, genuine, a hard worker, and very handsome.

My wish came true, and we became engaged and married two years later.

At the age of 33, Ken and I welcomed our first son; with our second son arriving only 18 months later. We were very busy, but our family was now complete!

It was only five and a half months after our second son was born, that I was lying in bed and found a lump in my right breast. I knew instantly that I would call and have it examined.

After seeing my family physician, he recommended that I have an ultrasound done, which was booked right away. The ultrasound showed a mass that the radiologist suggested we biopsy, which was done on the spot.

Now to wait two weeks! What a scary time.

I can remember the follow up appointment like it was yesterday. I was sitting in the office with my little guy in tow, when the physician said those terrible, nasty, hateful words, "It's breast cancer." Immediately my body went into shock, and I sobbed like never before.

I thought, "*There is no possible way this can happen! I'm 35, eat well, exercise, I'm a wife, and most importantly, a mother to two precious little boys!*"

I called my husband to break the news to him. Together we cried out of fear, but he picked me up and helped me to understand that we were going to make it through this.

Within a couple of weeks I had the lumpectomy surgery done with the removal of one lymph node. After testing the node, we discovered it contained cancer, so a second surgery was completed to remove more lymph nodes to check them. Thank goodness they were clear.

The surgeon explained that my diagnosis was stage 2 cancer. After a few weeks of healing, 8 rounds of chemo would follow, then 25 rounds of radiation. Losing my hair was minor compared to the thought of losing my life.

My body soon became unrecognizable to me, like I had never seen it before, and I didn't like it. At 5'11" I was very skinny, weighing in at 138 pounds. Chemo had stripped my body of any muscle I had. I felt rough and knew I needed to do something to get past this stage.

8 weeks after completing radiation, I met up with a girlfriend for a coffee date with our kids. She had mentioned she was doing CrossFit one night a week and that I should consider trying it out (I had heard of CrossFit but never gave it much thought).

I chatted with another girlfriend who was considering it as well, so we picked a date to start and away we went. I remember being extremely nervous with some serious butterflies in my stomach. I also remember showing up with my skinny arms and legs thinking, *"Well, here we go,"* not knowing exactly what I was in for.

The girls that day were fantastic and very welcoming. To them, it didn't matter that I was the new kid on the block, they were going to encourage me to complete the WOD anyway. I remember, during part of the strength portion, barely being able to lift the 35 pound bar overhead. What was I getting myself into?

The very first WOD we would do was the burpee ladder. It was torturous, and I sweated like I hadn't sweat in years, maybe ever. I left knowing that the next day would bring some significant pain, but also that I strangely loved what I had just done. After all those years of being an athlete, I had never experienced a rush even close to this.

Although I was proud I made it through my very first WOD, the greatest blessing that came was my "aha" moment where I knew that CrossFit was going to be my therapy to get through this! So back I went two days later, and then again after that.

I soon found that if I had to miss a class, I became annoyed. I was hooked. I talked about it to anyone that would listen, and I still do. Ken is also an avid CrossFitter, so many of our conversations are about new PR's and muscle soreness after our most recent WOD.

What CrossFit has done for me is miraculous.

These days, my recovery time after each WOD is minimal and I am steadily adding more weights to that 35 pound bar. More importantly, being able to turn a worrisome day (about a recurrence of the breast cancer) into a feeling that I can conquer the world happens at some point during each WOD. It's phenomenal what it does for the mind. The complete satisfaction of conquering a WOD now far outweighs the nervousness I feel on the way to one.

What I considered a hobby initially has now turned into a full blown obsession. I am proud to say that after a year and a half of going multiple times a week, I stand at a very proud 155 pounds, with my muscle mass increasing steadily. I have worked extremely hard to get to this point, and I'm excited to see where the next few years will take me.

Today, I am exactly where I am supposed to be. Almost two and a half years out, I am moving forward with my life, surrounded by those who mean the world to me. I am happy, strong, confident, and most importantly healthy. I live in a positive environment, where a substantial piece of my circle includes my CrossFit family, who have encouraged me to push myself more than I ever knew I could.

My recovery will be a lifelong journey, and CrossFit will continue to be a large part of it. It has challenged me, but more importantly it has empowered me. It has shaped how I think mentally and physically and I am stronger than I have ever been.

My goal is to continue to get bigger and stronger, and I know I will do it. I enjoy participating in community CrossFit competitions and my goal next year is to compete at the RX level. I have never felt this type of loyalty to an exercise program and enthusiasm in my life. Always wanting more.

I truly believe that this occurrence happened because I was too stubborn to realize myself that there was a more meaningful life awaiting me. It's as though I was picked up and placed into this new life that I should have been living all along.

I am extremely grateful for what I have left behind, as well as what (and who) I have met in the meantime. This new devotion for CrossFit and passion for this sport (and connection with this group, The Big Momma's) is unbreakable. The CrossFit community is truly like no other.

The camaraderie is both superior and inspiring. Having had the pleasure to WOD at different CrossFit locations, one thing is clear. The "box" location and programming may be different, but the message is the same. Being a CrossFitter means that you share a similar passion for the intense sport. But more importantly, it doesn't matter who you are, we will all support each other, sweat, laugh, and play together. We cry over our frustrations and celebrate our victories together. We are as enthusiastic about the first one to finish a WOD as we are to celebrate the last one.

After seeing what CrossFit continues to do for me, I would strongly encourage others to give it a try, as you too may become hooked and never look back!

*****

Aimee continues to train multiple times each week and has recently earned her CrossFit Level 1 Certification.

Story Fifteen

Ben O'Malley

In 2006, my client Adrian was involved in a serious road traffic accident. A reckless driver sped head on into his car as Adrian was making his way from work to collect his four year old son, who had leukemia at the time.

The collision was so severe that Adrian suffered life threatening brain, orthopedic, and abdominal injuries. In that moment, his life changed forever.

Robbed of an extremely prosperous career, his physical and mental health would require years of rehabilitation. A lengthy court case followed, then ultimately his marriage broke down and he had to leave the family home he shared with his wife and two children.

This is not news to me. I've written this scenario out many times, but that introduction never gets any easier to comprehend. Let's face it, if this was a work of fiction it would seem a little elaborate as a plot line and you'd be forgiven for questioning its authenticity.

Let me assure you, this is definitely real life and a harsh sequence of events that really happened. I can tell you this because I am a part of this story, but my involvement as Adrian's full time Personal Assistant appears during a much later chapter in his life, beginning in 2012.

My background to this story is, thankfully, less traumatic.

I'm Ben, Adrian's full time personal assistant and founder of the Monkey-Box. My experiences prior to this role have formed the foundational beliefs of my approach to supporting people, so it's important that I explain a little about these before we move forward.

I've always wanted to help people above all else but I've never identified myself with any of the traditional helping professions, although I have flirted with many of them over the years, amongst other stints as a punk band manager, grave digger, and construction worker.

As a teenager I volunteered to help people with learning difficulties, then in my late twenties I returned to the care industry as an Activities Co-ordinator in a mental health nursing home. Then I experienced the more specialized role of Brain Injury Support Worker, working with some very complex needs.

These experiences chiseled some very permanent etchings on my belief system and reaffirmed my identity as an alternative operator in an industry dictated by middle managers peddling financially motivated decisions and risk reduction practices that fail to address people's needs as human beings.

I'd grown cynical of the industry I was in and decided to leave for a job digging graves for the local council.

I'd left the industry, but here I had developed four basic values that have served me right in later life:

1. If people move better, they live better.
2. Support should be a collaborative experience.
3. People need a purpose to live well.
4. Purpose is synonymous with the concept of work and being useful to other people.

Skip forward to 2012. I'm on a break from digging a grave in the sun. My shoulder hurts and I'm considering a change in career. Whilst scanning a newspaper, I see an advert for a part time support worker and decide to arrange an interview.

It's at this meeting a week later where I first meet

Adrian and I'm offered the job as his personal assistant. He is amenable to my ideas, plucky and determined. His family are supportive and I finally have a genuine opportunity to exercise my values, minus the red tape and bureaucracy that had negated my ideals before.

Here was a life affirming opportunity, for both of us, it turns out...

Adrian had been having a difficult time dealing with the separation from his wife and with irregular support workers, and much of the focus from his life had naturally been guided towards his divorce and injury settlement, which was still going through the courts at the time.

We spent a year together before I was offered the role of his full time PA and here marked a new beginning for the both of us.

Adrian's physical injuries were severe and the rehabilitation process has been lengthy. He suffered over 50 breaks in his legs, causing his walking gait to be impaired. He is also partially sighted.

These considerations are serious enough alone to make daily life very difficult, but the addition of the frontal lobe injury has escalated Adrian's problems to another level. The brain injury is complex. His executive functioning is severely impaired, he has difficulty accessing stored memories, experiences chronic fatigue, and is registered epileptic.

Most significantly, he has lost the ability to initialize tasks, which is a major focus of my role with Adrian. Even with the best will to be productive, Adrian simply cannot initialize a behaviour on a regular basis unless it is part of a shared experience or he has been heavily prompted beforehand.

I set about our work together by developing a routine that would encompass the values I had formed in consideration of the difficulties Adrian faces.

Introducing structure was fundamental in the process and still is today. I began by introducing a rota for the month ahead, detailing daily events that replicated a kind of working week with tasks for us to complete together.

Then we set about trialling a number of activities each week that I felt would be physically and socially rewarding. These included going to a local gym, undertaking voluntary work with a local wildlife charity, swimming, outdoor fitness classes, DIY tasks, attending concerts and sporting events, and slowly introducing some more physically demanding challenges like walking Mount Snowdon in Wales then completing a half marathon later on.

We had built the foundations of a collaborative experience and we had achieved a monthly routine that had, in part, addressed the many voids left after

Adrian's traumatic experience. There was progress, but it wasn't as good as it could have been.

I felt that some of the major issues relating to Adrian's brain injury were not improving as I hoped they could. He still found it very hard to initialize behaviours and his mood deteriorated as soon as I stepped back from processes we had put in place.

Adrian was and still is very good at wanting to please others by appearing to be doing well when maybe he isn't. So what could I change for us? It was certainly true we were developing purpose and we had a collaborative support process in place. However, we hadn't achieved the other values I mentioned earlier.

Adrian wasn't really moving better than he used to, just moving more often, and we hadn't developed something that was directly helping other people. At least not to the extent that we are today.

Adrian was doing activities that encouraged him to move more often, but his ability to move well wasn't improving and I began to suspect that this was a contributing factor as to why, consequently, some elements of his brain injury were not improving.

I understood that some elements of his injury may not improve in such a short space of time and others may never improve at all, but my previous experiences with other clients had led me to believe Adrian could be doing better. We just had to find a new way forward.

I was looking for inspiration and it came in the form of a sport I'd never heard of until a friend suggested we try it. CrossFit. A combination of Olympic lifting, gymnastics, and metabolic conditioning. Here, I'd found a methodology that would enable us to move better than before because the coaching is very much centered towards improving range of movement, biomechanics and consistency using functional movements. More specifically, CrossFit involves compound movements that inherently enable large motor recruitment patterns — something I now believe is the primary catalyst for the development of neural pathways in Adrian's continued rehabilitation.

Months after joining our local box and immersing ourselves in the community culture the sport encourages, I was seeing a newfound motivation in Adrian, alongside significantly improved physical developments, which were also confirmed recently by Adrian's surgeon, who confirmed increased muscle mass, bone density and range of movement and a realignment of the right patella.

Much further down the line, we have seen significant improvements in Adrian's ability to initialize behaviours and episodes of chronic fatigue are extremely rare.

Prior to beginning this training, Adrian had been unable to initialize dynamic movements such as jumping or running, and chronic fatigue was a daily consideration. Knowing this, we wanted to develop the idea of functional fitness as support for complex needs and developed the Monkey-Box to develop our ideas and continue Adrian's journey.

Adrian and I decided to turn his garage into a fully equipped gym. The Monkey-Box. "Monkey" because we had come to realize that functional primal movements, such as lifting, carrying, pulling and pushing had become the tools of our support process together, and we wanted to develop an image to represent this.

We set about using the Monkey-Box as a laboratory to experiment with the fundamental movements we continue to learn at CrossFit Lutterworth. We went on courses together, and I qualified as a CrossFit level one coach. We went to college to become gym instructors and undertook kettlebell qualifications and completed nutrition courses. Additionally, I gained a British Weightlifting Coaching qualification.

We had built the foundations of something that would go on to satisfy the last missing value in our time together: being of use to other people.

Community is a big deal in CrossFit and I had always felt that people are the most important asset in any process of change. We began to widen our horizons by traveling to other CrossFit boxes around the UK, meeting coaches and athletes and sharing our story along the way.

Monkey-Box was on the road in more ways than one. We began to meet people who told us they were inspired by Adrian's story and as our work became more known in the community, I started to receive emails from people who were keen to learn about the Monkey-Box approach to support, and many from people with complex needs who needed help in their daily lives.

What had begun as a casual chat at the beginning of a workout, had quickly grown into a more elaborate seminar with Adrian and I carrying all manner of equipment with us to get our ideas across. A screen, a laptop, a projector, and practical demonstrations of movements. Even our own printed t-shirts, vests and hoodies to get the message out there.

We set up our website, monkey-box.net, and social media networks and began to keep an online record of people we met, places we visited and progress in Adrian's life.

Adrian had an outdoor rig built in his garden, complete with wall ball shots, Olympic Rings, and climbing ropes. During the summer we are able to take advantage of the leafy Warwickshire terrain, using farm trails and country roads for running and burden carries.

Suddenly we realized that the Monkey-Box had

become something much bigger than we could have imagined. Along the way we have been able to support people with varied complex needs, such as a woman who has a brain tumor, a young woman who suffered a brain injury after an assault, a man with a chronic abdominal condition, a retired engineer who has one leg and suffered a broken pelvis and complications following surgery, a woman who suffered a brain hemorrhage, and even a few seasoned athletes along the way too.

Every week I run a free-of-charge Monkey-Box Open Session for people who need extra help. We follow the basic principles of CrossFit programming and encourage others to access to the community through the work we do. We help people to move better as part of a community, and the results have been brilliant.

Today, Adrian has a very active life. He is part of a collaborative support process, he is moving better, he has purpose in his weeks and is part of something that helps other people.

Adrian's executive functioning has hugely improved; he is able to initialize behavior more often and episodes of chronic fatigue have been hugely reduced.

The Monkey-Box project and our involvement with the CrossFit community continues to evolve. I am coaching part-time at CrossFit Lutterworth. Our seminars across the UK are well attended and I am currently in the process of developing a course for the helping professions, *Functional Fitness as Support Level 1.*

I'm extremely grateful we came across the CrossFit community, and I'm even more grateful Adrian has given me the opportunity to develop the Monkey-Box project with him.

Adrian's story is one of success, tragedy, determination and hope, and at the time of writing this he is only 37 years old. This story is only just beginning and I'm more than excited to be part of whatever comes next.

Story Sixteen

Paula Irish

I was born with a rare condition called Poland Syndrome. Poland Syndrome is a disorder that affects individuals born with abnormal muscles on one side of the body.

Most people have abnormalities of the hand, which involves a smaller hand and shorter fingers. My right hand is smaller than my left and my fingers are shorter than on my other hand. When I was born, my fingers were webbed on my right hand and I needed to have a few surgeries to correct this.

Looking back at my childhood, I realize now that nothing stopped me and I lived a "normal" life. I grew up on a farm driving tractors and four wheelers. And now, in the wintertime, I enjoy snowmobiling. My cousin switched the gas lever and put it on the left side of my sled, so I have no difficulty riding. It's great because nobody else likes to ride my sled because of the switch!

In my teen years, I played on basketball and baseball teams. I just learnt to modify and make things work. It was what my friends were doing and I was not going to just sit back and watch. For playing baseball, I had a special baseball glove made to fit my smaller hand.

Fitness has always been a part of my life.

I was the type who would get bored very easy at all the gyms in the area. I did not like doing the same workouts every day. That is why I would not be a member at a gym for long; I always needed a change.

People kept saying to me that I would love CrossFit and I would always say, *"I couldn't do that. All they do is lift weights and I can't do that with my right hand."* I would always use my hand as a reason not to give it a try.

Three years ago, two of my friends finally bugged me long enough and I joined them at a Foundation class at Driven Athletics. I was actually worried that I would not be able to do any of the workouts, that they would have to modify everything.

The day I walked in, everyone was lifting heavy weights and doing pull-ups on the bar and what I thought at the time were some crazy workouts. I told my friends that I couldn't do any of these workouts with my hand, but boy was I wrong.

It started with the trainers modifying almost everything. This enabled the trainers to assess how much strength and mobility I had in my right hand.

In the beginning of my CrossFit journey I hated doing anything that had weights. I only liked the workouts that were just cardio. I would look online and see what the WOD was, and then if it was lifting, I would skip it.

Over time, the instructors were able to figure out what I could and could not do. This took a lot of trial and error and if it wasn't for the amazing trainers at Driven, I would not be where I am today.

In the beginning I could not do any workouts with the barbell, because I cannot make a fist and therefore I could not hold onto the barbell. However, I was able to push press. I would start from a rack, cradle the bar between my thumb and index finger, and push the bar over my head. So for a bit I would do just push press when the WOD had any weights. Then one class, the trainer came up with an idea of using a strap that I could wrap around my wrist and then around the bar so I could to do deadlifts, push presses, and cleans. I was very excited when they came up with that idea, and it worked great.

I began to feel more like I was doing what everyone else was doing and I was able to add weight and was no longer just using the bar. I may not be able to lift what everyone else is lifting, but I am getting an amazing workout. After every WOD I am usually flat out on the ground trying to catch my breath just like everyone else.

I now enjoy lifting weights as part of the WODs, which I never thought I would say. The other movement that took a bit of time to figure out was a pull-up. It was just one of those movements that I just wanted to say that I could do. It was difficult for me because I had a fear of using the pull-up bar. During a WOD with pull-ups, I would always modify to a jumping pull-up. I was worried about hanging above the ground. If I ever fell and injured my left hand, I would not be able to work or function because I rely so much on my left hand. So our gym purchased a bar called a Yolk. It stands on the floor and I can do pull-ups by using bands to help me without the worry of falling a big distance. I wrap a strap around my wrist and then around the bar and my feet can touch the ground if needed. I usually just bend my knees so my feet don't touch.

Joining CrossFit has been an amazing experience. It is a great community that I am proud to say I belong to. Everyone is so very accepting to the point where people don't care, acknowledge, or perhaps even realize that my right hand and arm are different.

Every person is very supportive and always there to cheer each other on, no matter what the fitness level may be. There has never been a day that I did not look forward to going to my CrossFit box.

Story Seventeen

Kimberly Caringer

Four years ago I didn't know what CrossFit was and I had never lifted a barbell in my life. Like many CrossFitters out there today, the story of what brought me to a CrossFit gym for the first time is an interesting one.

At the age of 29, I was diagnosed with Stage 2 breast cancer. It was a shock as I was so young and had been living a normal life with no previous health issues.

All of a sudden I had a life-threatening, aggressive form of cancer that needed to be treated fast. Why I would get cancer at such a young age was baffling to me as well as my doctors. I hadn't known of any family history and I tested negative for the breast cancer gene. But there was not a lot of time to think about why it happened to me; my focus and energy quickly turned to beating it.

After more than a year and a half of treatment that included chemotherapy, a double mastectomy, and radiation, I was happy to have beaten breast cancer, but at the same time I was left exhausted and physically weak. I knew I needed to get my strength back, but I wasn't sure where to start.

A friend invited me to a CrossFit class at a local gym called "244" in Tucson, Arizona. I didn't know what to expect and my first workout made me realize I was much weaker than I thought. I couldn't even do one proper push-up. But it was a turning point.

That phase of my life was over and I was ready to come back. I was instantly hooked. Every new task that I accomplished — whether it was a push up, a pull up, a little heavier clean — was a small victory.

Gym 244 had and still does have, an impressive coaching staff that welcomed me and embraced my fitness challenge. Included in this staff was coach and owner, Samantha Silverman. This beautiful, engaging 22 year old was a fierce competitive CrossFitter who grew to be a close friend and inspiration of mine.

Within my first few months at the gym, she told me about the organization *Barbells for Boobs.* This organization raises funds through the CrossFit community to provide breast cancer detection resources for those that need it, especially for young women under the age of 40 and men that may not have coverage.

I was immediately drawn to the cause and Sam and I committed to organizing a fundraiser at the gym for two consecutive years to support *Barbells for Boobs*. The energy and support surrounding these fundraisers were electrifying.

Sam was right there next to me as I did my first RX Grace, which is also the signature workout for *Barbells for Boobs*. I was cheered on by my newfound CrossFit friends, and those who had supported me during my recovery.

During these events I was able to share my story about how CrossFit had brought me back to life again.

Sam knew many of the *Barbells for Boobs* staff and was determined to introduce me to them personally. Sam saw the power my story brought to the cause and knew we could take it further and help more people along the way. Unfortunately, this introduction never took place.

On January 24th, 2015, Sam was tragically killed in a car accident at the age of 24. This shocking news rippled throughout the CrossFit community and left all of us at 244 completely devastated. The life and spirit she carried into the gym everyday was suddenly gone.

Coincidently, at her funeral, I was introduced to Zionna, the founder of *Barbells for Boobs*. I told her my story and how Sam had wanted to introduce us. After some tears and hugs Zionna told me, *"Well, she finally got us to meet."* Zionna asked me right then to be a community advocate for *Barbells for Boobs*, where I could continue to tell my story and keep Sam's legacy alive within the organization.

Since that time, I have had the opportunity to speak at the *Barbells for Boobs Pro Advocate* camp, meet and work together with the *Barbells for Boobs Western Region Community Advocates*, and have grown close with all the staff who work tirelessly for this cause.

Hearing the background stories of their connections to this organization continues to inspire me. I feel lucky to be a part of an organization committed to making a huge impact through social change.

Through CrossFit and *Barbells for Boobs*, I have been able to look back at cancer and know that I not only beat it but I have come back bigger, better, and stronger — both physically and as a person.

Zionna and I have agreed that as we continue to deal with the loss of our friend, our fateful introduction and now friendship has brought us some peace in that we know this is what Sam wanted.

*****

Kimberly Caringer now lives in Lake Tahoe and trains at South Tahoe CrossFit. Kim continues to be a Western region community advocate for Barbells for Boobs and plans to carry on annual Barbells for Boobs fundraisers in Sam's honor.

Story Eighteen

Miles Coleman

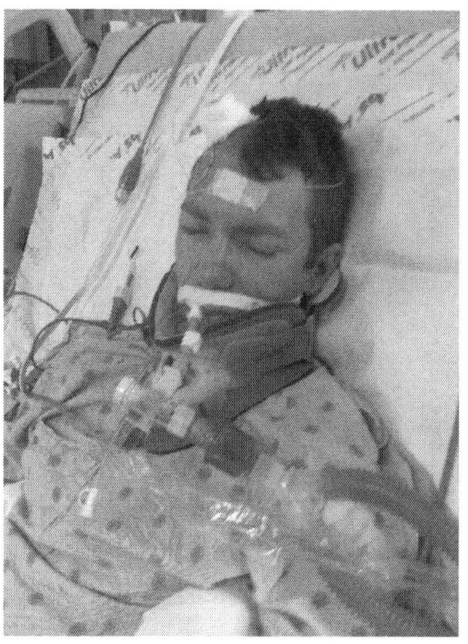

September 5, 2012 is a day that, in some ways, changed my life forever, and, in other ways — amazingly — hasn't changed it at all.

That morning, while preparing to coach the 5:00 am class at our CrossFit gym, I fell while retrieving the climbing ropes from the rafters and suffered a traumatic brain injury. I actually don't remember the accident, the preceding day, or anything from the following several days.

From what I'm told, however, the initial prognosis was fairly grim. The doctors told my wife there was a real possibility of death and, if I did survive, there would be fairly serious complications, like the inability to walk, talk, or remember anyone from before the injury.

They were certain I would never practice law again.

By God's grace, and against all the odds, the days and weeks that followed were a series of events that were nothing short of miraculous. Within 24 hours after the injury, the pressure in my brain rose precipitously and the doctors cleared the room and prepared to do surgery to remove a piece of the skull, which would be implanted in my abdomen to keep the skull fragment alive until it was reinserted.

Moments before they began, the pressure inexplicably subsided. The day following the accident, they removed the ventilator and I was able to say my name, my wife's name (which was a great relief to her!), and identify what city I was in and what year it was. The following day — two full days after the accident — I was able to stand and walk with assistance.

In total, we spent 11 days in the hospital, another two weeks at an in-patient rehab hospital, and nearly two months of outpatient rehabilitation services that focused on increasingly rigorous physical, occupational, and speech therapy.

Over this time period I still had headaches caused by brain swelling and impairments with visual-spatial processing and executive function skills. I also came to realize I couldn't smell or taste, nor could I hear very well out of my right ear.

Apparently, if you hit your head hard enough, you can actually sever the nerves that connect your olfactory and taste receptors to your brain, and you can dislodge the tiny bones that connect your eardrum to the hearing nerve. My ear was surgically reconstructed and now works fairly well. My ability to taste and smell, however, has not yet returned.

While I don't remember the accident or the initial parts of the recovery process, I learned a number of valuable lessons over the months of rehabilitation and the gradual return to work and working out.

First, life is short, uncertain, and unpredictable. Don't waste it.

I had a fantastic job, a wonderful wife, was successful, young, and in great shape. But in an instant, all of it was almost taken away. Make the most of the time you have and be intentional about your priorities. For many of us — including me — it is easy to devote ourselves to work with hopes and good intentions of spending time on our kids, marriages, and other pursuits later.

In my case, in the month immediately prior to my accident, I logged the highest number of billable hours I've ever worked in a month. I worked every weekend and almost every evening.

Looking back following the accident, I thought several times how glad I was that that had not been my last month on earth.

It's good to make plans, set goals, and work hard. But remember, in the words of the New Testament: *"You do not know what tomorrow will bring. What is your life? For you are a mist that appears for a little time and then vanishes."* Life is short. Don't waste it.

A second lesson I began to learn is that I was simultaneously dispensable and indispensable in different ways and to different people. After my accident, I was out of the office for nearly three months. During that time, none of my clients lost their appeals; no files were neglected; nothing fell into disarray. It was soberingly easy to compensate for my absence. The truth of the matter is that I was professionally dispensable.

In other aspects of life, however, my absence would leave a void that was much, much harder to fill. Remember: You can and someday will be replaced at work, likely without too much difficulty. But you are indispensable to your family. Your presence, time, and attention is irreplaceable to your spouse and kids.

Make your highest priorities the places where you matter the most, and spend your best time and efforts on the people to whom you mean the most.

Third, in trying times, keep the faith. I cannot over-emphasize the significance and the comfort that my wife and I found in our faith during the period we were dealing with my brain injury.

There is extraordinary peace in knowing there is a divine and providential hand guiding our circumstances, even when they seem chaotic. That no matter the outcome, all would eventually be made right. That regardless of circumstances, we would be given the strength to persevere.

Finally, be physically prepared. Nobody works out in anticipation of or in preparation for a brain injury or other traumatic event. But when such an event occurs, it certainly helps to be physically well prepared.

Of course, when life's challenges arise, being physically well prepared won't make them easy, but it will make them easier. Sometimes we know certain challenges are coming, like having a baby or the inevitable process of aging, but other times we don't.

In either case, being physically ready will make them easier to handle and recover from. Whatever sort of exercise or fitness regimen you choose, it should be something that you enjoy, something that progressively challenges you, and something "functional" that mimics real life.

*****

Following his recovery from the accident, Miles returned to practicing law. He still coaches CrossFit and participates in CrossFit training (though he took a brief hiatus from climbing ropes following the accident). After recovering from his brain injury and regaining his strength, Miles has PR'd all his lifts and named WODs. The only lingering effects of the accident are an inability to taste and smell due to severed nerve connections, senses that may or may not eventually return.

Story Nineteen

Anna Coleman

On September 5, 2012, I was planning on working out at the 5 am CrossFit class that my husband coached. I was dressed, had my shoes by the door, and at the last minute, decided to stay home and go back to bed. I had a headache and thought I should rest before going to work for the day. My husband, Miles, kissed me goodbye, told me he loved me, and headed to the gym.

Twenty minutes later my phone rang. I glanced at my phone and saw that it was a friend from the gym. I assumed she was going to harass me as to why I wasn't at the gym, so like any normal person would do at 5 am, I ignored her phone call. She then texted me, *"Anna, please pick up your phone."*

I sensed something was wrong, and that this wasn't a joke.

I called her back and could tell her voice was shaking. She told me I needed to get to the gym as soon as possible because Miles had been injured. I was still trying to process what she was saying and didn't fully comprehend how serious it was. I asked what was wrong, and she said Miles had hit his head and needed to go to the hospital. I asked if he would need stitches. Clearly, I didn't have a clue as to what had just transpired.

I got up out of bed, put my shoes on, and found my keys. I drove to the gym, anxiously praying it wasn't anything serious. When I arrived, an ambulance was pulling away. Some of the guys from the gym took my keys and ushered me to another vehicle.

I got into the car of one of the gym members, Ryan, who was a doctor. He asked me for my phone and asked who he should call to meet us at the hospital. I was starting to realize this was more serious than just stitches. I was confused and asked him what he meant. He said, *"You should probably call his parents and any other family members and tell them to come down immediately."* I looked at Ryan and asked him if it was that serious. He said yes. I asked him if Miles was going to die, and he said, *"I don't know."*

We arrived at the hospital and several of the CrossFit members arrived as well. They started to tell me what had happened that morning.

While Miles was getting the class warmed up, he sent

them out for a 400-meter jog. The WOD included rope climbs. Miles was going to get the ropes down that were stored up among the rafters when not in use. As he had done countless times before, he jumped from a plyometric box to grab a loop of the rope that was hanging down slightly from the rafters. While hanging on with one hand, he was using the other hand to wrestle the rope down from the rafters. Somehow, his knee got tangled in the rope and he lost his grip, flipping him upside down and falling about 12 feet to the ground, where he landed directly on his head on cement.

They didn't tell me he was unresponsive or about all the blood he had lost. But I could tell by their faces and tears in their eyes they were shaken up but trying to be supportive. Thankfully, the class that morning included two doctors, several nurses, an EMT, and a firefighter, and as a result, Miles had been able to receive immediate medical attention.

Miles was placed in ICU and it was several hours before he had stabilized and I could see him. I vividly remember walking into the ICU room and seeing him hooked up to a ventilator and a probe coming out of his brain. The doctors and nurses were all talking and trying to explain to me what was going on. I didn't hear them. I was still in shock, staring at my husband who was currently in a coma and non-responsive.

This couldn't be real, I kept thinking...

The nurse handed me a stack of papers to sign, and at that moment I broke down and lost it. I was trying to process what was happening but still couldn't wrap my head around it.

Miles suffered a traumatic brain injury from the fall and as a result had a fractured skull, severe swelling in the brain, and two hematomas. I walked over to him, held his hand, and told him I loved him and that everything was going to be ok. I barely recognized him and asked for him to squeeze my hand. Nothing. No response.

They ushered me back out to the waiting room, and I still was in a state of shock. The doctors came out and began to explain that the next 24 hours were critical. They also explained that if Miles did survive, he would most likely have serious complications and there was the possibility he might never walk or talk again. They were certain he would never practice law and warned he could lose his memory, including his memory of me.

I suddenly realized how my life was probably going to change forever.

I remember walking out of the hallway and not being able to breathe. Two of my friends embraced me, and our pastor came over as well. I don't remember much from that time, but I do remember our pastor saying, *"All you need to do is remember Jesus loves you and Miles."* The words were simple, but true and comforting.

The One who created the world out of nothing loved me and had my best interest in mind, even in the midst of this horrible situation. I knew ultimately that Jesus loved Miles more than I did, that He would do what was best for both of us, and that I needed to trust Him.

Over the next few weeks, miracle after miracle occurred.

The doctors thought they would have to do brain surgery on Miles to relieve the pressure, but moments before they began, the pressure subsided on its own. Miles was responsive that same evening by squeezing my hand. The next day a therapy dog — who happened to be a Great Dane, like our two dogs — came to visit. I leaned over and told Miles there was a dog that had come to visit him. He lifted his hand up and placed it on the dog.

A few days later they took the ventilator out of his mouth; they asked who his wife was, and he said my name. Three days after the accident, a physical therapist came down and Miles was able to walk. The doctors were astounded and nicknamed him "Miracle Miles." They had never seen someone with such a severe brain injury begin to recover so rapidly.

We spent 11 days total in the hospital and then went to an in-patient rehabilitation hospital. After spending two weeks at in-patient therapy, we were able to go home. Once we got home, Miles was able to slowly resume his normal activities. He continued outpatient therapy for an additional two months and then was cleared. Amazing!

Over the weeks and months of Miles' recovery, we were so blessed by the help and support of our family, friends, church, and — of course — the CrossFit community. The group of people in that 5 am class helped save Miles' life, and the support and assistance of the two physicians from the class was invaluable during Miles' hospitalization.

We are grateful for them, and they will forever be part of our lives. Other gym members sent cards, brought meals, and rallied around us to ensure we were being taken care of. They encouraged Miles when he came back, and pushed him physically and mentally to regain his strength.

CrossFit is more to us than a just workout. It is a group of people who come together to support each other, not just through a difficult workout but also through a difficult season in your life.

Story Twenty

Julie Sherman

On a seemingly typical Saturday morning, while participating in a group WOD, I caught a partner wall ball leaning too far forward. At the time, I had been attending graduate school for my Master's degree in Exercise Science and Health Promotion with a newly started internship at the CrossFit box.

I had struggled with back issues for 10 years at this point, which included severe back pain and complete numbness down my right leg. The pain during this particular wall ball felt different. Later that evening, when I woke up in the middle of the night to a wet bed, I knew that it was serious. I immediately called my sister, who works in the healthcare field, and was frozen with fear at just the mention of the word "paralysis."

I packed up my stuff that week and moved back home to see a surgeon. He confirmed I needed a spinal fusion (L5S1). During our unfortunate conversation, I mentioned wanting to be able to squat 200 pounds again. His response? A simple affirmation: *"You will never be able to squat again. Maybe this whole working out thing isn't for you."*

I'm an athlete, who has worked out almost every day and sometimes twice a day. At the time I was a personal trainer. I loved to spend hours just hanging out at our box, whether it was completing a WOD or helping to train a fellow CrossFitter. Needless to say, my whole world was crushed. Actually, it seemed like it was falling apart right before my eyes.

For the sake of my health, I went through with the extensive surgery. For months afterward, my life was filled with very hard to abide by restrictions. I had to wear a back brace, couldn't bend over, and couldn't lift more than five pounds. I couldn't even do my own laundry.

Every day I struggled to get out of bed.

Little successes came in the form of showering myself

and tying my own shoes. Each morning I forced myself to walk a half mile. Upon completion of my walk, I would be so exhausted I'd get right back into bed and need to rest for a few hours.

Thankfully, my friends, family, and CrossFit community were incredible through the entire experience. They showed their support by visiting me in the hospital, bringing me food, and sending me inspirational cards. My best friend even reached out to Christmas Abbott, who sent me a postcard that read, *"Keep the drive for life alive. Your passion will shine through the darkest of days."*

As soon as I was cleared to drive, I'd visit my CrossFit box, *CrossFit Tried and True*. During these visits I watched my teammates strive to reach their goals, which made me feel alive again. With the support of my team behind me, I eased back into working out.

About five months post-surgery, the most weight I'd cleaned was 65 pounds. The strength portion on this particular day was a clean and jerk so I set a safe, however ambitious, goal of 85 pounds. My coach and I agreed that I wouldn't split jerk in case my back arched. 85 pounds.

Boom! Seemingly pretty easy, actually.

I looked at my coach, he smiled, so I threw some fives on. 95 pounds still felt good! As everyone was putting their weights away, he said, *"Do you want to give it another try?"* I thought he meant 95. I automatically said, *"Sure!"* Then he slapped 2.5 pound weights on. At this point of 100 lbs, the weight went up nice and easy. Well, maybe not perfect, but as nice and easy as it can be after not working out for five months. This was huge!

Five months prior, I was told I'd be "lucky to lift a hundred pounds again." A few days later, I completed a three rep body weight front squat of 125 pounds.

It was during my recovery time that I made my first three trips to volunteer in Haiti. I volunteered and lived in an orphanage, which didn't even have crayons to use for the coloring books we had brought. They had some of their basic needs met: food, shelter, and education. However, the orphanage was lacking play and, more importantly, love.

Back home, local CrossFit boxes had donated jump ropes, bands, and rings for me to take on my trips. I was hopeful and eager to share our love of fitness and health with the people of this third world country.

The boys at the orphanage loved practicing bar muscle ups with the bands, and the girls played for hours with the jump ropes. In addition, I was also able to find two "gyms" on the island. Let me clarify. By "gym," I mean, an outside space with old, rusted curl bars, a leg press, a dip station, and a few odd dumbbells.

I went to Haiti with zero ability to speak their native language, Creole. Therefore, introducing the equipment I brought with me was quite a challenge. At the same time, it was also an awesome opportunity to become familiar and work with the locals. I formed incredible relationships through fitness, which in turn resulted in English-Creole tutoring, learning about our dissimilar cultures, and ultimately, great friendships.

It was during the very dark time of my back surgery, that I realized I had a purpose in life: to help others. My purpose was and is not to make millions of dollars, or put up the best Fran time at the box. Rather, my purpose is to use what God has given me to help and inspire others.

I continued to do CrossFit while I was home in between my Haiti trips. I also formed an organization, *Just One Haiti,* to educate, inspire, and empower children and families. My organization provides children with the opportunity to attend school, while we work with their families to help them obtain jobs to sustain their own families' long term needs.

Another calling: This past August I donated approximately 70% of my liver to a man in need. The workout restrictions were intense once again. I was not allowed to train for months after my surgery. At my routine three month appointment, they found a hernia in my diaphragm. This resulted in another surgery, which really put me behind in terms of recovery.

Honestly, I still get frustrated that I'm not near where I used to be athletically. I just remind myself that the struggle is part of the challenge and it's fun. Every day I feel that struggle but I feel blessed that the struggle is within me. I will overcome my struggles. In turn, I'm determined to help others' overcome their own struggles. Every day is a blessing. Every day is an opportunity. Every day we are blessed with God's Grace. What you do with it, well, that's your decision to make!

*****

Julie is currently living and working in Haiti serving orphans and vulnerable children. She has committed to live and work for the next year in the Orphanage run by Calvary Chapel Church of Port-au-Prince, and also to serve as a mentor for children who've been rescued from child slavery through the efforts of the Restavek Freedom Foundation.

A Note From Kelly Graham — I have several headbands that Julie makes and sells on Etsy to raise money for Just One Haiti. One headband provides enough money to educate a child for two weeks. They are comfortable, fun and full of hope; you can check them out here: http://ittakesjustone.etsy.com

Story Twenty-One

Michelle Pauze

"Every day she rises before the sun to train. She strictly regiments each aspect of her diet, and she studies her competition in minute detail. But ultimately, her success comes down to her own concentration and execution. To the cheering crowds, this race looks like a moment of effortless skill. I, however, know that it is the culmination of years of training and commitment that few in the world can match. Win or lose, that is her true triumph." ~ Author Unknown

I was an "in-completer." Let me be clear, an in-completer is not a failure. I never failed at anything because I always found something to move onto before failure. I am not a quitter; I would just see a better opportunity to move on to, leaving the past incomplete.

In 2000, I became friends with someone who would

not only inspire me to complete stuff, but someone who taught me more about tenacity, believing in myself, and believing I had the ability to succeed.

The truth is I had known and looked up to Kelly Graham long before we became friends. In eleventh grade Kelly began teaching at my high school. I knew she was a great athlete and I considered myself an athlete as well, so I was elated when, years after my high school graduation, we became teammates on a provincial ball hockey team.

It wasn't till 2008, when I learned of some life changing health issues I was having, that I would understand the extent of the friendship I had with Kelly. Although very active and involved in many sports, I was 100 plus pounds overweight and my eating habits were terrible. I was stuck in a job I hated and felt the weight of the world on my shoulders.

From the very moment I confided in her, Kelly took me under her wing and began to teach me how to train for life and not just the now.

We began a daily routine of food journal emails, walks that became runs, and working out at the gym, all the while developing a friendship that was unlike any other I have ever known. She could motivate me with just a stern look that would simply say *"JUST TRY."*

Her vocabulary did not include the phrase "I can't," and whenever I would bellow out those words, they fell on deaf ears and I would press on and push through, realizing my body was more capable than my mind thought.

Even during the times I felt I was holding her back from the training she was used to, she was always the encourager. I would apologize to her for having to "dumb down" her regular 10km run to a much slower "5-ish" kilometer walk/run and as she ran backwards or sideways or skipped or lunged along, she'd contentedly say *"exercise is exercise,"* all the while pushing me further and further each time out.

Then one August she started going to this new gym and suggested I try it. I immediately declined and refused to go and even test it out. In true Kelly fashion, she would then do double daily workouts — one at her new gym and a second with me. Finally, after four months of this I succumbed to her request to "just try it" and in December I went to my first CrossFit class.

I HATED IT!

Joanne, the CrossFit coach, did a follow-up call with me a week after the class and I told her plain and simple I would not be back. I explained that the biggest reason was because I could not do a pull-up nor would I ever be able to and I did not want to go daily and experience the frustration that accompanied my inability to achieve what looked like a fundamental CrossFit movement.

No matter how hard both she and Kelly tried to explain how unimportant a pull-up was to the overall positive benefits of the CrossFit training, I was dead set against ever returning and stubbornly refused to listen to any reasoning that would convince me otherwise.

Then I found myself at Christmas time, 70 pounds lighter and with a wonderful, clean bill of health — except that at that point I had plateaued. I still wanted to fit into a little bit smaller clothing and no matter what I tried nothing seemed to work.

Kelly had helped me so much up until now and I was still unwilling to trust her about the benefits of CrossFit.

When I was able to recognize the ridiculousness of this, I showed up to the CrossFit box with an attitude I can only attribute to having learned from Kelly, and I dove headfirst into the now exciting world of CrossFit training.

As Kelly immersed herself more and more into this fascinating world, I tried to do the same but sadly, the old self-doubt I felt would creep back and I would delve back into my own pity party. Kelly was always right there to snap me back into reality and encourage me to push on, not to worry about impressing anyone but to be the best me I could be.

To date, my favorite CrossFit highlight was competing with/against Kelly in a UG Beach Competition, and although the field was small, we stood together on the podium, she with the gold and me with silver.

Kelly has pushed me to be a better person. She has shown me how to start something and see it through to COMPLETION, not only by how she has poured herself into my life but more importantly by the example she has set in her own. Lifestyle speaks louder than words and Kelly's lifestyle exemplifies her drive and determination, and anyone in her circle can learn from her example.

For the first time in my life, I have completed something. At age 43, I have graduated from college and am about to embark on a career. Kelly has stood by me and encouraged me to be a stronger person. She has taught me that if you are willing to put the work into it, success is there waiting and is completely attainable.

She has shown me that no matter how dark things seem, there is always a light waiting to shine through and sometimes I just need to dig a little deeper to find it. She has shown me with her own life that incomplete is not an option, and for all this and more I am forever thankful and appreciative of my friendship with her.

No amount of words can ever come close to expressing what her friendship means to me.

Story Twenty-Two

Everett Sloan

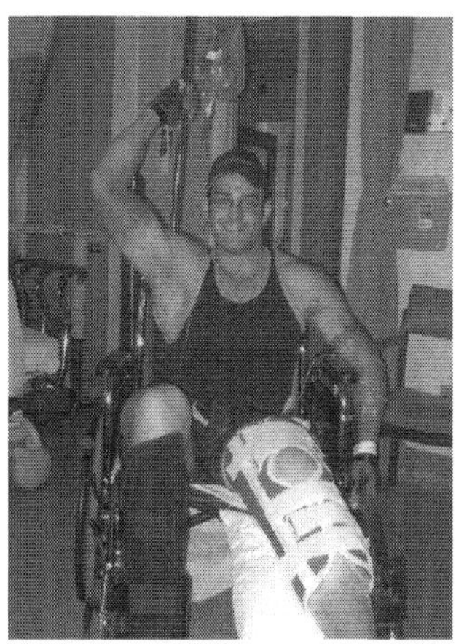

I grew up as an identical twin in the country. We were adventurous and physical our entire lives. I remember playing almost every sport growing up. I must have driven my parents crazy, as every year I wanted to try something new. Like many children of the 70s and 80s, I grew up idolizing the action heroes like Sylvester Stallone and Arnold Schwarzenegger.

I started bodybuilding as a teenager to try to emulate the physiques I saw in those movies and magazines.

I did this for many years, with a passion for bodybuilding coming in waves. I sometimes left bodybuilding to pursue strongman or powerlifting. They all seemed repetitive and fairly one sided for fitness. I always felt I was missing something and I wasn't sure if this was something I would continue for the rest of my life. I also enjoyed any and all outdoor hobbies that involved physical activity.

One of those hobbies was motorcycle riding. I was pretty good at it and after a short time, was already doing well on the track and would go on adventure riding tours across the country. While playing around in a sand pit, I had a pretty severe accident when landing a jump.

To spare you the graphic details, it was readily apparent that my legs were badly broken. After some time and many surgeries, I was told I would probably never be able to walk properly again, and definitely could never squat again. During the healing process I had several major complications and my outcome was looking even more grim.

I had a lot of time to think while I was in the hospital. I thought about what I was going to do with my life if I couldn't walk. After four months in the hospital and in and out of physical therapy, I started back at the gym. I discovered I was pretty unbalanced and very weak. The passion just wasn't there. I wanted to get healthy and to just try and resume a normal active life, like being able to go up and down stairs and walk without a limp and extreme pain. I started researching functional training. This is where I discovered CrossFit.

I started implementing some of these, new to me, exercises into my daily training. After about three months of doing this in a regular gym, I was told to "stop" by the gym management. So I purchased some equipment and started training with a couple friends in my basement. This lasted about a year until my neighbours started complaining about the very early morning noises coming from my house.

My wife and I joined a local affiliate. At the time, there were only a few in the city. I quickly fell in love with the sense of community and the positive changes it was making in people's lives, physically through accomplishments in the gym, and mentally in their personal and professional lives.

After about a year of training at a local affiliate, I decided to give up my day job and open a gym in the city center, which was underserved. Three years and three locations later, my wife still has to tell me to come home every day.

I am truly passionate about helping make positive changes in the lives of others.

I have always been interested in philosophy, mainly about what impact I will leave on the earth. I have volunteered as a Big Brother for many years, and I try to be a positive influence on my son. I see the physical changes in my clients, but what makes me really happy are the changes I see in their confidence and life outside the gym. This is the impact I am glad to leave, people who are better at life in general and will live longer, happier lives.

*****

Everett owns and operates ***CrossFit Bytown*** *with his wife, Stephanie, where they concentrate on functional fitness and proper mobility in a fun, community-driven environment. He enjoys being a positive influence on his son, Mikko, and is heavily involved in keeping youth healthy and active.*

Story Twenty-Three

Amanda E. Turner

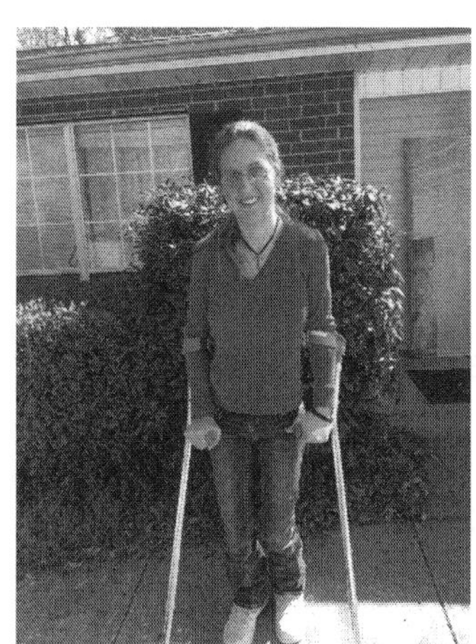

"We will either find a way or make one." ~ Hannibal

This is a quote that sums up my drive for life. I was born five weeks premature, which resulted in my lungs being underdeveloped. As a result, my brain did not receive enough oxygen.

When I was three years old I was diagnosed with spastic diplegia cerebral palsy. This type of cerebral palsy impacts my voluntary skeletal muscles. My fine and gross motor skills are also impacted. I have difficulty with things like walking, maintaining my posture, and penmanship.

Growing up and into early adulthood, I attended physical and occupational therapy to help me overcome the deficits I experienced as a result of cerebral palsy. Attending various therapies, I learned to walk and improved my ability to maintain my posture. I was fitted for leg braces and used a walker and forearm crutches for ambulation.

When I was four years old, I was finally strong enough to walk independently.

One place where I excelled was academically. I attended public schools and graduated high school in 2001 at the age of 18, with some assistance. After high school, I decided I was going to move two hours away from home and attend Louisiana State University (LSU) in Baton Rouge, Louisiana.

In 2005, I graduated from LSU with my Bachelors of Arts in Psychology. In 2008, I graduated from LSU for a second time with a Masters of Social Work.

While at LSU, I worked hard to make the campus accessible for people with disabilities. I had used a wheelchair on and off throughout my life, but due to the size of LSU's campus, I began using a wheelchair full time. As a result, my legs became weak and I lost the ability to walk independently.

After completing my Master's degree, I worked as a social worker in Baton Rouge for a short time before accepting a job closer to home in Lake Charles, Louisiana. My professional background has been in the areas of medical and psychiatric social work.

Shortly after moving, my path crossed with a longtime family friend, Lindsay. She was a marketer for a local home health agency, so we would see each other frequently. On one of her visits she made it clear to me that she wanted to talk about more than just marketing. She began to tell me about a group called *Ainsley's Angels*.

Ainsley's Angels is a group that pairs up people with disabilities with people who are not disabled (who are referred to as angels), with the goal of promoting inclusion. The angels assist the people with disabilities to be able to participate in endurance events, such as 5k's to marathons and triathlons.

I told Lindsay there was one problem: I did not have transportation. She told me she would take me. In November of 2012, Lindsay picked me up and off we went to my first 5k race. Before we got out of the car, she said, *"Let me make one thing clear. I don't run, I just bake."* I thought to myself *"We will see! (haha)"*

I became very involved in *Ainsley's Angels*. In November of 2013, at my one year anniversary race, as a friend and I approached the finish line, she asked if I would like to walk across. I remember thinking I have not walked since I graduated high school in 2001. When we got to the line, I remember holding another friend's hands and dragging my feet across the finish line.

In January of 2014, I became the first person with a disability to participate in the Louisiana Marathon Series. This was my dream because the race went through LSU. My angels and I completed the half marathon. At the beginning of February, I completed another half marathon in New Orleans with *Ainsley's Angels*.

That weekend I shared a hotel room with my best friend, Michelle. It was at that time that I asked her to push me in the Louisiana Marathon in January 2015 (this would be my first full marathon). She said, *"okay, but only if you walk across the finish line."*

Fast forward to the end of February/beginning of March, 2014. I received a Facebook message from Lindsay. It basically said, "*When are you coming to the box with me?"* She had been participating in CrossFit for the past several months. I responded I would go to the box with her if she would do a 5k with me.

On Sunday, March 9, 2014, Lindsay picked me and my wheelchair up, and we headed to the box. When I got there I met Coach Meg and her husband, James. We spent the next hour experimenting and seeing what my body could do. I thought this was going to be a one time deal so I should enjoy it while I could. Meg had other plans.

Towards the end of the session, Meg asked me what my goals were. I responded that my goal is for Lindsay to run a 5k with me. We made arrangements for me to attend CrossFit twice a week. I had told Meg I had forearm crutches and she told me to bring the crutches and leave the wheelchair at home. I went home and I thought about my goals. I returned to the box the next day and told Meg I wanted to walk again.

I began working hard, week in and week out, to walk again, and eventually walk without crutches.

At this time, I was not happy with my weight so I began to adjust my daily nutrition. As I write this story, thanks to CrossFit and my lifestyle changes, I have lost somewhere between 40 and 50 pounds.

As my fitness improved, I began to set more goals. I asked Coach Meg to compete in an *Ainsley's Angels* race with me. In July of 2014, Meg pushed me for four miles, but she told me I had to walk across the finish line to her, unassisted. We had been practicing this at the box. I successfully walked across the finish line to Meg. Later that same July, Lindsay (the one who introduced me to *Ainsley's Angels* and CrossFit) and I competed in our first 5k together. That's right, she can no longer say "I don't run, I just bake."

In October of 2014, as a part of *Ainsley's Angels,* I signed up to participate in the Ethel Pretch 3k. I wanted to give a birthday present to my best friends, Michelle and Kristine (*Ainsley's Angels* Vice President) so I decided that with Michelle and Kris by my side, I would walk a mile in the race using my crutches.

It was a warm October day when we started the race. We walked and sang *'Roar'* and *'I Can Only Imagine'* as we crossed the finish line. By the end of the race, the whole community had filed in behind us, and we crossed the finish line together. I not only walked a mile, I had walked 1.4 miles.

A few months later, I would walk across another finish line for the New Orleans Saints 5k, holding Kris' hand. Finally, in January of 2015, I would return to the Louisiana Marathon and, with the help of Michelle, we would complete my first full marathon. When we got to the finish line, I stood up out of the jogging chair, grabbed Michelle's hand and, with Rooster, the President of *Ainsley's Angels,* and other friends by my side, together we walked across the finish line living out our motto of "**Yes You Can.**"

Every time I enter the box, I feel normal and accepted by all those around me. When I was younger and attended therapy, I did it knowing that this is what people with disabilities do, also knowing that I could not go to the gym like "normal" people.

Now when I attend CrossFit, I know it is a place for

everyone no matter their ability level. I have also learned that if you give it a chance, it just may change your life. You see, when I first entered the box, I thought this would be a fun two hours a week. I didn't really believe it would completely change my life outside of the box.

I was given a thorn in my flesh...Three times I pleaded with the Lord to take it away from me. But he said to me, *"My grace is sufficient for you, for my power is made perfect in weakness."* Therefore I will boast all the more gladly about my weaknesses, so that Christ's power may rest on me. That is why, for Christ's sake, I delight in weaknesses, in insults, in hardships, in persecutions, in difficulties. For when I am weak, then I am strong.

~ 2 Corinthians 12: 7b-10

*****

Amanda continues to participate in CrossFit weekly. She is working as a Licensed Clinical Social Worker at an outpatient mental health clinic in Lake Charles, Louisiana. Amanda continues to participate in races with her local chapter of Ainsley's Angels.

Story Twenty-Four

Brad Fewson

I began my life in the military as an airborne paratrooper in the Australian Army. I served on operations in the jungles of East Timor, chasing and fighting militia to ensure the country's freedom. I later joined our state police force and the Tactical Squads. Riots, domestics, car chases, arresting offenders, drug crime, and violence were all in a day's work. It fueled me and gave me purpose.

But still not enough—I took a job working for the U.S Department of Defense with the U.S Marines as a private security contractor. I left for Iraq and I went back to war. Two tours over two years of combat, firefights, car bombs, roadside bombs, terrorism, corruption, death and killing. Oh, we saved and changed lives as well, and to me, that was really living.

Living life to the extreme but making a difference.

I returned home from Iraq to my wife and children. Then I immediately left again to return to East Timor with the Australian Army for more jungle operations. I was looking forward to the adrenalin rush, the excitement, the uncertainty.

Then suddenly, every part of my being crashed. I couldn't relate or fit in with anyone around me. I couldn't concentrate, I became depressed, angry, suffered from nightmares and I had a constant fear of losing my family. I got pulled out of operations and sent home.

So there I sat with everything crashing down.

Twelve years of living life on the edge, pushing myself to the limits, mind body and soul...The military and the physical performance of my body was all that mattered to me and it was my living, but it was all coming to a crashing halt.

I sat in a medical office on a cold day in late 2008 as the Army doctors and physiotherapist told me the news. I needed surgery, there would be no more sports or impact work and I would have to look at changing jobs, maybe even an honourable discharge. My days of being a soldier and what felt like my purpose in life were over, life on the edge was catching up.

I had the mobility of a brick, riddled with injury. I was told the discs in my back required surgery. L4/L5/S1 were bulged and impinged the nerve. I also had degenerative arthritis in my vertebrae. My ribs were displaced which placed stress on the intercostal muscles and on my heart.

My world was in a spin. I had a beautiful wife of eight years, two beautiful children and close family and friends, but to me none of that mattered. I couldn't see past my work and though I didn't want to admit it, Post-Traumatic Stress from combat operations in Iraq and East Timor was raging hard within me.

I had been using exercise and work to deal with these stressors, and now those avenues were being taken away from me. My personality and experiences taught me to never give up, I had a vast array of life-changing and limit-testing experiences and I wasn't going to let some damn "minor" physical setback stop me.
I craved a tour of Afghanistan, and the Special Forces (SF) was my best option. My wife made it clear; if you must go, it will be with the Army, not done privately. I went harder into my fitness and work. I ignored the pain and dosed on prescription drugs. The toll on my body was immense. I had two suspected heart attacks and two trips to the hospital.

After a year of preparation, heartache and pain I got

selected to SF. Just two weeks later, my back totally went. I was out, really done this time, and right back to where I started. My doctors began the process of organizing the surgeries which they felt were necessary on my back, and started to realign my ribs to help my chest and heart.

I was told once again that I would lead a life of permanent pain, there would be no sports and fitness and I would also struggle with debilitating PTSD. Ultimately, my marriage was on the rocks as I was an angry man.

My wife and I separated... And then along comes CrossFit.

In my quest to avoid surgery at all cost and knowing I had to get mobility and movement back, I researched endlessly and just happened to stumble upon CrossFit. I saw how ordinary people were able to develop speed, strength, mobility and flexibility. It was ridiculous!

CrossFit wasn't known in many parts of Australia in 2009; it was still a seemingly underground movement but I threw myself at it...I needed to re-teach myself how to move and move with correct technique above all else.

I avoided surgery, I got mobile, and I got fitter, faster and stronger than I ever had...My relationship with my wife was back. I got qualified in my LV1 and PT courses and created a fitness company. I was so invigorated and fresh of life, and for the first time in a long time, I didn't need combat to feel that!

It had been such a long time since I had been excited about anything! If I could avoid the knife and heal my PTSD with CrossFit, then I could do this for a living. So I opened the first CrossFit coaching facility in country NSW, *Mil-Fit CrossFit Wagga*, and said goodbye to the Army.

My passion was infectious. Every member of my family became CrossFitters, from age 6 to 60.

Individuals wanting to coach, people just looking to begin a fitness program, and competitive athletes started to gather with me. The community craved coaching, rehabilitation and fitness. We introduced CrossFit Kids, went into schools and worked with government teachers in fitness courses and rehabilitation education.

Instead of taking life, I was changing and healing life. CrossFit healed my PTSD so I wanted to do the same for others. I created the MIL-FIT adaptive athlete program. We provide free training for anyone from the services, military and emergency response personnel, for those with PTSD like me. I wanted to train with people like me and heal them...and it worked.

In 2013, my wife and I went to the CrossFit Games for

our first holiday together in 13 years. Our marriage was strong again. Our CrossFit business was our life, seven days a week. We had 12 great coaches and a booming membership and it all operated whilst we holidayed. Life was GREAT.

But then it changed... At 35, at my peak of fitness, my body just stopped working. I would train, but my legs were always weak, like the muscles didn't want to work. Joints would hurt greatly, and my hands would fumble when lifting and grasping. I became forgetful and had trouble concentrating. Deterioration progressed, bringing muscle spasms, twitches and dystonic/chorea movements. I ignored it for six months, but then I collapsed.

Lesions on the brain... Subcortical neurological movement disorder...Traumatic Brain Injury from the combat and military life...

Over the following months, I continued a decline whilst the doctors struggled to pinpoint the problem. My body is my life, and once again, it had betrayed me. For the second time in my life, doctors and psychiatrists stated that my life as I knew it was over, deterioration was just a matter of time and acceptance of that was necessary.

After 12 months, I was classed as fully disabled, unable to work again, my driver's license was suspended, and I was told that I had no choice but to stop exercise/CrossFit.

Depression, suicidal thoughts, and alcohol became the norm. I had seizures nearly daily and there were days I couldn't walk or lift due to fatigue. My autonomic system has been greatly damaged, and I'm hypoglycemic daily. The medical world can't decide yet between genetics, multiple sclerosis, motor neuron disease or chronic traumatic encephalopathy.

Only time will tell...

Regardless, I had to get out of the hole and it was CrossFit that saved me before and it is CrossFit that is saving me again. My family has refused to let me stop. The coaches and the members of the CFW box community refuse to let me stop, my friends that battled PTSD with CrossFit refuse to let me stop.

Time and again they have supported me and brought me back to training, and constantly they would tell me that what they see is inspiration for everyone. They are seeing from their friend and coach that an adaptive athlete never quits.

Whilst I continue to battle this disease/disorder, it is the CrossFit community that keeps the light shining. I do not know what's in store for me, I have good days and bad, I can't run well and don't lift or move like I used to, but what I do know is that my passion for CrossFit that I have shared onto thousands of people has now been returned to me tenfold.

CrossFit saved my life, it gave me hope, freedom, family and happiness and it is continuing to do so. I live by the motto *"Pain is Temporary... Pride is Forever."*

*****

Brad Fewson is the director, coach and athlete from regional NSW, Australia's first CrossFit Box, www.crossfitwagga.com.au. He is also a teacher for fitness personal training certification and advocate for fitness and health for the disabled, mentally ill and veterans.

Story Twenty-Five

Krystal Nagel

I remember thinking over and over, this isn't my life. I was an engineer with a university education and a successful career in finance. I had prided myself on being mentally and physically strong in tough situations throughout my life, but here I was, terrified of my husband, afraid for my life, living with constant threats and physical intimidation.

I knew deep down I had to get out of this abusive relationship or risk it costing me everything, but I had been manipulated to the point of accepting what was happening and I felt so alone. I was constantly being torn down for something: my ability to provide, my driving, my post-baby body.

Everything I said, was, and did, was fair game.

When my son was seven months old, I started the journey that eventually led to reclaiming my life by getting into a self-made routine of lifting and bodyweight exercises. In this process, I discovered CrossFit. When my son was a year old, I joined a local CrossFit box and I instantly loved it.

It was at this point in my life where I began to feel that I could reclaim a little space, a little time for me.

This is something that is hard enough for all parents of a small child; however, my husband took it to extremes. He asked me to remove most of the evidence of my existence, my books, trinkets and clothes, from the main areas of the house as well as our bedroom, forcing me into less and less space, which made it nearly impossible for me to go out other than for work.

That little hour carved out of sleep before work in the morning, in that safe space, made a huge difference. I had accomplishments, increases in strength and skill that no one could diminish. I had a place where people really cared if I showed up and were happy to see me.

Most days during the WOD, I could shut out all the noise in my head, my husband's criticisms and threats, and my ongoing internal debate over what to do and how did I let myself get here. It all went away with 3, 2, 1, GO! That little hour in the morning gave me the boost I needed to survive the rest of my day and if everything went terrible, I still felt like I achieved something by surviving the WOD.

This place of support and the physical strength and changes I experienced gave me more confidence and the desire to change things. Unfortunately, my husband also noticed the changes and began to try to put an end to it. First, he was negative, critical, and dismissive of CrossFit. When that didn't work, he would stay out all night and into the next day so that I couldn't go to the gym because I had to be with our young son, and so I was forced to give it up.

It took me down for a while, but then I started doing CrossFit-inspired workouts at home. The support and encouragement I had received from the coaches and the community had begun to restore my faith in humanity and undo the abusive programming I was receiving in the place I was supposed to call home, with the person who was supposed to support and encourage me the most out of anyone.

It took time to find a way out, but by the time my son was 20 months old, I knew his father couldn't take care of him while I worked after seeing evidence of neglect. I realized that his verbal attacks on me at night were leaving my son shaken and sleepless. I enrolled my son in daycare and I knew that telling my husband that would be very dangerous. I was right. The night I told him what I had done, he attacked me and pinned me to the stairs. When I screamed, he put his hand on my mouth and my throat. I fought hard and eventually got away, only to wind up trapped in the bathroom with him breaking through the door to grab me again.

This time when I got away, I ran right out the front door, barefoot down the street through freshly fallen January snow until I found someone who let me in to call 911. I know that he chased me outside, but I never looked back to see for how long. If it weren't for CrossFit, I honestly don't believe that I would have had the speed, balance, reflexes, or confidence to get away from my husband's attack that night.

After the assault, I continued to workout in my home. I began using exercise to get through the stress of dealing with the legal process of divorce, and the criminal court proceedings. I got stronger all the time, but was left with significant emotional scars, hyper-vigilance, fear of new people, new situations, loud noises, and crowded places.

Last year I was able to join a CrossFit box again, and being pulled into the community pulled me out of my self-imposed isolation.

Having the coaches believe in me made me believe in myself, and constantly surprising myself by doing what seemed impossible, made everything seem possible.

One of the first weeks I was there, the class was doing front squats. The weight of the bar came down on my neck. I felt as though I was back on those stairs with my husband's hand on my throat. I was on the verge of tears, having a flashback in the lifting room. After some advice from a coach, I went to open gym time and stood there, racking and unracking the weight, until one week it didn't make me want to cry, and the next time, I didn't zone out and eventually I got to the point where I had one of the better front squats in the gym and I didn't give it a second thought.

Although at times things seem hopeless, things will, and do, get better.

For me, I now feel that I am less jumpy, more open, more relaxed, but I also know that what I experienced will always be a part of me. CrossFitters talk about going to the dark place to finish a WOD and in workout 14.5 of the Open, I found myself there. I wasn't feeling well; I realized the next day that I had the stomach flu, but at the time, I just knew that this WOD was tough and I was struggling. Suddenly, as I pushed through the discomfort, my mind went to a place where it wasn't the WOD any more. It was me physically escaping my abuser with my son, and I just kept going as hard as I could.

I think there was a little part of me that viewed, and maybe always will view, CrossFit as training to be prepared for the worst, but the Box is also my happy place. Sometimes it's a place to hide out and lift things until whatever is stressing me goes away, but always it's a community where I feel safe and supported and empowered in a way I never thought I could.

*****

Krystal still works in finance but is also a survivor advocate, speaking, educating, and advising on domestic violence from a survivor's perspective, and leading the SAFE doors initiative to provide safe spaces in the homes of survivors. Find out more here: www.facebook.com/SAFEsurvivoradvocacy

Story Twenty-Six

Kate Pankhurst

CrossFit increases your physical prowess across agility, strength, accuracy, balance, clothes shopping... er, what was that last one again?

My name is Kate Pankhurst, and I'm 53. I've been an obese child, teenager, young woman and adult. On long cycles, I've also been relatively small. The small phases coincided (occasionally) with falling in love, but (more usually) with being in a broken-hearted heap of tears at the exit of some loser boyfriend. I guess that identifies me as an emotional eater: stuffing in the pies while happy, eating nothing at all when miserable. But then it works the other way round for me too, which makes me a confused eater.

Either way, for a sedentary magazine designer, I ate too much...

In my time, I've grazed through most of the fad diets. I remember wearing cheesecloth tent tops in the '70s while nibbling through Cambridge Diet chocolate bars and wearing bat wing tents in the '80s to attend Weight Watchers.

The Cabbage Soup diet of the '90s was so awful, my memory is wiped of fashion. Needless to say, none of the above worked for long. If I was lucky, I'd go down a dress size and be totally euphoric. Then I'd squeeze every button and seam off the thing, and have to slink back to the shops six months later for my old size. Is there anything more dispiriting for a girl?

One boyfriend declared that he liked stick women with breasts, "like two fried eggs on an ironing board." I wonder now, why I didn't wonder then, what the hell he was doing with a spherical girl built more for comfort than speed? But for better or worse, I took the remarks to heart.

Like many big women who'd lost hope of ever changing, I tried to become invisible and gradually disappeared under loose tops and skirts (black, of course). I tried to make my huge boobs disappear with M&S "bust minimising" bras. I looked like a Stealth Bomber in lipstick. The boyfriend wasn't fooled, and he left anyway.

Some time later, I saw a programme on *Big Beautiful Women* (known as BBW's) — huge ladies who revel in their voluptuousness, eat with abandon and are worshipped by thin, pale men. It was a revelation! What the hell — I've failed miserably as a dieter — I might as well celebrate my body as it is.

Out went the tents and out came the cleavage and high heels. I was 5'3" tall and 15 stone, eight pounds. Woo hoo! But for me, it was a happy time, to have some body confidence, even if my body wasn't regulation model proportions.

Little did I know things were about to change radically.

It was summer 2007. Around this time, Andrew started teaching me to swim (as a fat kid, I never learned to swim, roller-skate or ride a bike — too embarrassing). On the way to the pool one day, he asked me what size I was. Straight out, just like that! Hiding my indignation at such a personal question, I confidently replied "I'm an 18." Actually I wasn't so confident — it was a lie. That day I'd bought a size 20 top and loose pants from Evans, the shop of shame once known as 'Evans Outsizes,' which have flowers all over their carrier bags, but no other identifying logo.

Casually, he started talking about CrossFit and the Zone Diet. We'd discussed it before, and I found it quite interesting. *"If I start doing this CrossFit thing,"* I said, defending my tenuous allegiance to the BBW movement, *"I won't loose my womanliness, will I?"*

I got some info on the Zone — and decided it was way too complicated with all the blocks and grams, etc. But I did get the message to eat more vegetables and treat rice and pasta with caution, so I had a vague stab at it. There were less ready meals and jars of sauce in my fridge, and I found myself cooking more. After a month or two, I emailed Andrew. *"I seem to have gone down a dress size and gone up a bra cup size. What are you doing to me?"* It was true.

That day I bought my first ever ever pair of jeans and a belt. Size 18, so no longer a liar. The belt was huge, and I was on the last hole (waist size 44"), but it didn't matter. I was wearing jeans! I wore them to work, and there were compliments. I felt fantastic.

Over time, some equipment started arriving at my flat. An 8kg kettlebell and some hand weights. My apartment block has nine floors, so my first workout was being made to do five triceps dips in reception, walk up nine floors, and then do five push-ups. I nearly died of exhaustion. Each day I did a bit more: puffing and blowing like a horse, I swung my kettlebell, did thrusters with hand weights, climbed stairs.

2008 went by in a blur of shopping and recycling! It seemed as soon as I got into one size, I was out of it and down to the next. I was either buying stuff in New Look (jeans only £10!) or taking them to charity shops. My jeans belt seemed to have more hanging out the front than was going around me, so I got a new one. I lost three stone and three sizes.

The compliments were coming thick and fast from my work colleagues.

I photographed CrossFit London events, learning as I watched. My tiny flat now had an Olympic bar and plates, along with a pull-up bar and bands. I went up through the kettlebells to a 16kg. I went running. I stomped up and down thousands of stairs.

2009 was harder. I suppose the regular weight loss had become addictive, and I was disappointed to be stuck at size 14. Then it was pointed out to me that stabilising your weight is as important as losing it. Think about it — if you never stabilise, you're in danger of piling the weight back on, and when you reach the so-called "goal weight," you need to be able to stay there.

Perseverance paid off, and in 2010 I lost another two dress sizes. Hang on, what does that mean exactly? Every woman knows that dress sizes vary from shop to shop. Another stick for women to beat themselves — we all want to be a Ghost size 8, not an M&S size 8 (which I just know is bigger). Well, I say to hell with it, go to the shop that encourages you to feel good about yourself. I am currently a New Look size 10 (stretchy) jeans, and an M&S size 8 top.

I hope this doesn't sound like one of those stupid (lying) adverts about miracle easy weight loss stories. For me, it began easily and got more difficult, and I've still got a long way to go. I've discovered through CrossFit that I'm quite strong (early on I deadlifted 90kg, and am still dining out on the story) but that I'm pretty crap at anything gymnastic. But then CrossFit makes you challenge your weaknesses.

In two-and-a-half years (I think a sustainable

timescale for radical change), I've shrunk my waist by 12" and lost a whopping five stones in weight. My blood pressure has plummeted from the 150s to 120/70. I'm faster, fitter, happier — and my buddies are beginning to describe me as "sculpted."

A quick note to all you BBWs out there: If you're happy being big, that's fine (you are gorgeous, empowered women!). On the other hand, if you suspect you may simply have given up in despair at ever getting slimmer and healthier, then there is something you can do. Give CrossFit and the Zone a try.

I've since quit my office job, got my CrossFit L1 Trainer Cert, and now teach CrossFit. My clothes are all made by Nike and Reebok! I've changed my mind and attitude to my body a few times in my life: from despair to denial to acceptance and finally to reform. This is where I've been for eight years, and where intend to stay!

"Vain trifles as they seem, clothes have, they say, more important offices than to merely keep us warm. They change our view of the world and the world's view of us." ~ Virginia Woolf, Orlando

Story Twenty-Seven

Michael Choi

Normally when we think of community, we think of communities that tend to be loosely involved by their planned group activities or outings rather than understanding member's interests.

In contrast, the CrossFit (CF) community is unique and different in such a way that athletes have a deep understanding of the common attitudes and interest of the community. One could argue a reason for this understanding stems from the terminology used within the community.

To any outsider looking into the CF community, they would be baffled with jargon such as thrusters, PR'd, Rx'd, and EMOM. To members it makes sense. Such as, "Karen" would be a typical female name, but to members, it rings the thought of sore legs and the high fives that ensues afterwards.

I would almost say this jargon is analogous to an ethnic community where membership is granted by speaking the language and that is the "glue" holding the community together. Except the bond in the CF community is fitness, and the jargon reinforces the community understanding of the workouts and movements.

Additionally, I can personally attest, as someone who has walked this earth and dropped-in at various boxes in different countries, no matter what the local language is, the CF terminology and goals are universally understood.

With this understanding, members of the CF community are almost always willing to help other members with their fitness needs, despite sometimes never meeting face-to-face.

There's one instance of this community accord I fondly remember and was proud to be part of.

I received an e-mail several months to the start of the CF Open WOD from a fellow named Erik. He was from Stockholm, where he lived and studied. He made plans prior to the start of the Open WOD in 2012 to visit an old friend in Barcelona for a weekend, which happened to coincide with an Open WOD announcement.

During the weeks leading up to the start of the Open WOD, Erik realized there would be a schedule conflict with his trip to Barcelona. Each Open WOD was announced at 5 pm Thursday Western time in the States, which was 2 am Friday morning for Erik. Under normal circumstances, Erik would normally hit the open WOD during the weekend and submit his scores before his local Monday 2 am deadline.

However, for the 12.4 WOD, Erik's departing flight to Barcelona was 6 am Friday morning. Therefore, Erik couldn't perform the WOD at his usual box with his home crowd cheering him on. Instead, he had to perform the WOD in Barcelona.

Erik wasn't too worried; after all, there should be people in Barcelona that CrossFit with plenty of boxes to be found, right?

Well, after an internet search, Erik came to the dreadful realization that there was no box to be had in Barcelona. The nearest advertised box to Barcelona was a three hour train ride west of the city. At this point, he started fretting and thought about his options for submitting a score for 12.4.

After vigorously searching more on the internet for nearby boxes in or near Barcelona, Erik stumbled across a blog post written by me about the lack of CF affiliates in Barcelona. Some readers wrote comments speculating when a box would open or provide alternatives gyms.

He was hoping that CF Barcelona would open in time for the Open WOD. He sent me an email detailing his desperate situation, to see if I had any more specific updates with Crossfit Barcelona.

To this day, I remember reading his email. The tone of

Erik's email had a sense of determination to submit a score and a hint of desperation when he actually contemplated doing 12.4 between the time the WOD was announced and his Barcelona bound flights, which would be between the hours of 2 am and 6 am – not exactly anyone's prime time to work out.

I didn't have any information about the opening dates of CF Barcelona. What I did have was a contact, Dan at a Reebok affiliate in Barcelona, and I reached out to him because he would have a better idea. I wasn't exactly buddy-buddy with Dan – I've only known him virtually. But with Erik desperate as he was, I wanted to help out any way I could.

I replied to Erik stating I couldn't promise anything, but I told him I had a contact over in Barcelona working at Reebok. After all, I didn't know if Dan was CF level 1 certified or not, but I was hoping Dan could help Erik.

Fast forward a few days...

I received an email much like this from Dan, stating that he could judge Erik for 12.4 at their staff box:

Hi Mike,

Things are going well, I had a meeting with the new Box owner a few days ago and he said he is planning to be open in May. Did you see the recent Reebok commercial? There are two large red boxes beside my office ready to be moved to locations in Barcelona. Feel free to give your friend my contact. We have some athletes from the UK dropping by this weekend and are doing the first Open WOD in our box.

Keep me posted.

I relayed the message to Erik; he was ecstatic and felt a sense of relief that he wouldn't have to hit 12.4 in the wee hours of the morning or even worse — fail to submit a score for 12.4

Erik's e-mail response sums up the community involvement well:

Thank you very much!

It is astonishing, really, what we will go through to get a workout in, and how others like you and Dan give so generously of your time! I am looking forward to meeting Dan and completing 12.4 at his box. I will forward you pictures and notes as soon as I get back to Sweden.

Thanks Again!

Erik brought a CF shirt from his home box as a gesture of goodwill for Dan's hospitality at his staff box.

To any outsider of the CF community, they wouldn't understand why completing the WOD and submitting a score was so important. To members within the community who understand the "Open WOD" and what it represents, it's important to complete all the Open WODs not only for fitness itself, but also for the completion of involvement in the 2012 Open.

I felt that's the reason why I went to the extra effort for Erik to submit a score for 12.4. Being a participant in the 2012 Open WOD myself, I too would have been disappointed if I had a big fat "zero" for 12.4, especially if the reason was simply that I couldn't find a box to be judged at during my workout.

The moral of the story could be not to schedule any travel during the Open WOD, but I think it clearly shows how the CF community understands the interest of its athletes so much that athletes are willing to help others despite never meeting face-to-face.

I feel the CF community understands fitness and goes beyond just encouraging each other to work hard during our workout, which is why Dan and I felt compelled to do everything in our power to help Erik submit a score for 12.4.

I'm probably not far off in saying that if Erik was in a position to help another member submit a score for an Open WOD or just drop in for a workout, he would be more than willing to help. I have no doubt this attitude causes a cascading effect, thus making a stronger community.

Story Twenty-Eight

Nina Sugamori

I was sitting in my Jeep texting my ex-boyfriend in tears about my arm and my accident. He was confused. *"Were you just in an accident? Or the one before?"* Of course he was confused! It was 2010 and my really bad car accident was in 1983. I had just left the CrossFit Level One and was determined to deal with my reconstructed arm differently, and it made me cry like a fresh wound opening again.

You see, at the age of 20, I was hit by a drunk driver while riding my motorcycle at Venice Beach, California. My right arm was shattered into multiple pieces and reconstructed with three stainless steel plates and 15 metal screws. I underwent 10 surgeries while I was still in college.

From 1983 to 2010 [27 years], I had dealt with my shattered, maimed, reassembled arm as a non-focus. Nothing could be about the arm.

Everything must be about what I have left. Then, when I began CrossFit, I needed to refile this idea. I needed to say, okay, lets see what this arm can do, and it was upsetting. But I was ready. I thought, I want to do a pull up. "They" say moving loads is from your core to extremities. I am so literal in how I interpret words, I thought this meant I could do this!

Oh! And the other detail regarding my attending the CF Level 1: I hesitated to attend because I wasn't whole. My arm was missing a radial nerve, a bicep, a tricep head and an inch of bone. My boss, Ronald, and his friend, Victor, said, *"Ya. Just go. There might be guys in wheelchairs there from Iraq."* And so I was like, *"Oh, what am I crying about?"*

I spent the next five years working everyday at *CrossFit Mean Streets*. I learned a huge lesson. I thought my arm was limited because of what was missing. What I learned was what was wrong with my damaged limb was also wrong with MANY whole uninjured people. What I learned from Stacey Hallerces, the trainer and physical therapist there, was that issues with extremities are often from the joint above the limb. So I began to really consider the position and usage of the scapula and how it relates to the arm as well as the core and posterior chain.

I watched everyone every day. And even a doctor that trained there persisted in lifting very heavy weights despite knowing his upper crossed syndrome was not being addressed! He was an educated, active person with means. I began to realize that what limited me was my focus and my understanding of my situation, not my accident or my missing parts.

I saw healthy young people struggle with movements others learned easily because their shoulder blade position and balance of strength was unevenly developed. There were also many limitations caused by ankle or hip flexibility. The scapula alone was ultra important with so many repetitions of weight overhead or ring dips and pull-ups and push-ups.

So I learned to snatch up to 60 pounds and even went to an Amateur Athletic Union Weightlifting and Powerlifting meet in 2015. I snatched and cleaned and deadlifted. My 215 pound deadlift placed me first for women age 50-54 weighing 53kg or 117 pounds. I can rope climb and do a pull-up.

Working at Mean Streets and in a CrossFit environment also taught me that competing was normal and, depending on the person, a healthy goal to set. So I prepared for a figure competition for females over the age of 50. In 2014, I took five first places in two organizations and in two states. I adopted the lifestyle of competing. It kept me focused on future goals. It is healthy for me and brings the best out in me. It exposes me to inspection and can encourage others to improve themselves too.

I liked that CrossFit, Inc. increased the number of fitness characteristics from the previous five to a list of 10. Then I realized that to be successful at CrossFit, a person needed even more than these 10 parameters. They needed mental resolve, higher processing of information, a mastery of food management, and enough control over their lives and stress levels to make room for excelling at physical pursuits.

I worked on food preparation, applying Kitchen Karate techniques, and I improved everything about how I did things and how I presented myself and managed my life.

I began to really embrace that food was more important than exercise. I spent so much thought and energy reworking my personal food preparation and recipes that I ended up cooking 90 meals a week for myself and 10-15 members at my gym. It was all grain free and with many vegetables. I came forward with raw cocoa, sugarless super food beverages and protein gelatins and many things that made people scratch their head! It was very adventurous and fun.

At the five year mark, I have achieved wonderful results. I am engaged to marry the love of my life. My training and cooking skills will keep my family fit now. I will help as many people as I can manage food better with Diet Free Life methods from my new home. This is basic macro nutrient targeting with insulin spike reduction, paleo or otherwise.

I can absolutely, unequivocally state that CrossFit changed me and my life with great depth and lasting effects. I hope to live a long time and share this with others.

Story Twenty-Nine

Shelli Gardiner

As a teenager I was sucked into that pull of being cool and started smoking. I continued to smoke until I was around 39 years old. I finally smartened up and quit.

After quitting, of course, the weight followed. I am not one who is okay with carrying extra weight. I started running. I ran my first half marathon when I turned 40. Six months later, I had an AVM, a sister to a brain aneurism. I survived an extremely close call with death. I am still living, BUT it caused me to have a massive stroke.

There are too many things to list that I've had to relearn. Not to exclude basic things like how to sit in a chair again. In my intense rehab they realized I had "left neglect." I wouldn't respond or see things that were in my left vision. I don't recall certain things, but my family tells me I would walk into a wall that was on my left. I could not see the left side of a page and would start writing in the centre of the page.

When I was discharged from the rehabilitation hospital, I was transferred back to our smaller centre that doesn't have as intensive a rehabilitation program. Still, I continued to get better. A therapist's job is to get you on your feet. Then you are on your own. I didn't think I was done getting better and stronger. I wanted to work on my strength and fitness.

After I received some rejections from other gyms in our center, I approached the local CrossFit gym. I spoke to the owner, Evan Lindsay, to see if he would be able to help me. He said he would give it a shot. The first day I walked into the CrossFit gym was with my cane. When I look back on that first day, I was a very weak, lost woman.

After years of being my trainer, Evan told me his thoughts that first day. He knew he took on a big challenge and wasn't exactly sure what he was going to do to help me. He also confided with me that he thought I was barely conscious when I came to the box. I was told repeatedly I was a mess!! The first thing I realized about going to this gym, was that they focus on your movements, trying to get them better.

There has only been positive results from working out in this gym. Previous therapists would see me out and about and comment how strong I was getting!! Evan noticed I was "walking" but not "stepping," so we focused on this movement, over and over until it clicked for me. Together we figured out a way for me to get down and back up off the floor. He was concerned if I fell how I would get back up again?

Then we did it CrossFit style: I would get down and get back up as many times as I could in a certain time. Before, during and after my WOD. A big fear with stroke people is how you get back up. I now can get down then back up like popcorn. My husband has completely stopped worrying about that. Evan brought back muscles I didn't even know I had lost!

Shortly after, Scott (my husband) and I were in the bathroom. He pushed me aside. He started laughing as I didn't wobble like before. *"Well, I guess I can't push you around anymore!"* It just wasn't getting me strong again that Evan gave back to me. He gave me hope. That was the biggest thing for me. We became good friends. Even after a massive stroke, I could still go on and live my life.

Understandably, most stroke victims lose friends. As Evan worked with me in the gym, I was gaining friends daily. Everyone wanted to see what we were achieving together. Of course I talked about CrossFit all the time, just like everyone else who joins. It was just my WODs were different than the regular classes. Soon after my husband joined, then we took our daughter on buddy day. Now our whole family CrossFits.

The family that CrossFits together stays together!

Life is funny how it shapes up. My husband and I are now the proud owners of the CROSSFIT GYM!

I will continue getting stronger and gaining new friends. Life isn't fair BUT keep smiling because it is worth the smile. I believe Scott's and my smiles will be the strongest muscle in our gym.

Story Thirty

Brianna T

"What's happening? What is going on? I don't want this, get off of me. Please stop, please just get off of me, I didn't want this, stop, no, no, no." He finished and climbed off of me.

I awoke face down in a pillow, fully clothed, tights ripped off down to my knees. He didn't even bother to take them all of the way off, probably scared I would wake up before he could accomplish his task.

This isn't the first time I've come to or woken up with a man, but it's the first time I wasn't blacked out drunk and it was the first time it was with someone I knew, someone who I thought loved me, who I thought I loved, and it was the first time I remember fighting someone off of me.

It had been just another drunken night of drama with Chad, fighting about who knows what. I went to his house so that we could talk and sleep and cuddle. He told me he loved me this time and just wanted to hold me, to fall asleep with me. I ate these words right up; I was at my lowest point mentally, physically, and spiritually. I had not one drop of self worth and his words were like an oasis in a desert that I had been wandering around in my entire life without any water or food in sight.

I met Chad a little over three years before that night. It was closing time at the 211 and I had drank more than my fill. I had just turned 22 and my sweet ex-boyfriend didn't show up to my party the few weeks before, so I had been drinking and sleeping around "at him," trying to hurt him but instead it was killing me. I had already ruined that relationship with my need for the drink and my inability to trust anyone who treated me with kindness or respect.

So it was closing time and I was introduced to a charming blue-eyed boy with a killer smile, and the next thing I knew we were taking a cab to my place. More darkness as I was in and out of a blackout, then I woke up feeling absolutely awful with this guy in my bed next to me. I was already at the point of accepting that this was my life, such a sad thing to accept as normal. I was so uncomfortable and wanted him to leave but he wanted more so he took it; it wasn't quite rape but it was degrading and it was hurtful.

I didn't think I had a voice, or that I deserved anything more.

So that was the beginning of our relationship. It was up and down and back and forth and there was a lot of cheating on new boyfriends and girlfriends and each other. He became more forceful and used more flowery and lovey words to get me to come back to him, and I was completely trapped, so sucked into his world, he was like the alcohol I consumed...so abusive and making me hate myself, but I thought I needed it for my survival.

When I was finally able to look at him, he looked just like it was any other day, any other sexcapade, no big deal. I, on the other hand, had been bawling and I asked him why, why did he do this? He simply said to me, *"I couldn't help myself; you're just too sexy and you were there in my bed, you turn me on too much."* Like it was a compliment to be taken like that by him.

I believed him. I really, truly thought that since I was in his bed asleep that it was just what was going to happen. I was so sick and so full of self loathing that I thought I was only worth being used for sex, that since he was so turned on and attracted to me (mind you, I was 140 pounds of solid fat and alcohol, swollen and slightly yellow from booze consumption, and I wasn't a fan of the shower or eating), then I must have deserved it.

That meant something about me; I was worth something as long as a man wanted me, especially if that man was Chad.

It took me a number of months to finally hit my total bottom and realize that I needed to get sober (June 24, 2010 is my sobriety date). I never told anyone about Chad and I never, ever uttered the word "rape."

Until one year into my sobriety, sitting on my

sponsor's couch doing my sex inventory and we finally got to Chad. I told her the story and she said, *"so he raped you?"*

"Oh no no no, he didn't rape me, I knew him. He was sort of my boyfriend, I was in his bed."

"You said no, you told him to stop, and you were sound asleep when he forced himself on you, inside you. That is rape."

Wow, I let those words sink in for a minute. She was right. He did rape me. Denial is a powerful thing and this realization of what I had kept hidden for those two years hit me like freight train. I sobbed and shook, and she held me and told me I was going to be ok. That what he did was wrong and I never had to see him or talk to him again. He was not an amends I was going to make, no matter what.

Fast forward another year and a new sponsor. I still had not done any work on being raped so when I saw Chad for the first time, I completely flipped out. I tried to hide and cover my face with my hood, like it was all happening again. So we did some more work. I went deeper, looking for my part in this whole thing.

I originally thought my part was that I was there in his bed (I deserved it) when I shouldn't have been. I thought that my part was still too big and too much about making myself wrong. She gently showed me that I did not deserve it, I never did. She pointed me to my part, that when I am in my active alcoholism I go there, to that place where I surround myself with the lowest of the low people, that I can't accept any kindness or love, only pain and abuse from myself and others.

To know that this is the disease, it breaks me down, takes away my choices. I have no choice, no voice, no control the minute I put alcohol into my body.

2013, I decided, was the year of no fear — the self-centered kind of fear, the kind of fear that has held me back from thriving my entire life. I was going to seek humility and grow closer to my God. I had just ended a relationship with a man who was a predator. He never raped me, but he definitely put a lot of pressure on me sexually and in other areas of my life, trying to control me and my son.

I was 115 pounds soaking wet, skinny and with big boobs. I had the body I always wanted, the one I thought would make me desirable, the one I would starve and over-exercise to get. I hated it. I hated this weak body, the one that a predator would find attractive and easy to take.

I looked up my old friend Dan's Spokane Valley CrossFit website again (I had been on the site more than once over the last five years, coming up with reasons and excuses why I couldn't). I read about humility and that it was needed in order to start CrossFit, that "anyone could do it but it wasn't for everyone."

I felt like God had just spoken to me right then. I called Dan and he told me to come in and workout once for free. I went in, I asked God to come with me and I felt like a little girl holding hands with her parent as I walked into the box that Thursday night to meet Dan.

He wasn't there; I panicked. Then I remembered "year of no fear!" I said these words to my higher power, *"God, I offer myself to thee. To build with me and to do with me as Thou wilt. Relieve me of the bondage of self, that I may better do Thy will. Take away my difficulties, that victory over them may bear witness to those I would help of Thy Power, Thy Love, and Thy Way of life. May I do Thy will always!"*

Then I let the coach tell me what to do, and I did it. I talked to people, I met Adrienne and we talked about food, how great it is, how we eat so much, and we laughed, hard, and I came back again, and again and again. I could only afford the $5.00 Saturday class at first, so I showed up every Saturday for a month until my tax return came.

When I saw Dan finally, he was shocked by how skinny I was. He signed me up for a two times a week plan because I was scared still and I am pretty sure he laughed because he knew. He knew I was hooked already.

I met 'Brookie Bear,' another of the coaches, during one of my first mixed classes, when she patiently went over some olympic lifting with me after class, took some videos, and sent them to me (I felt so cool). She was shy then and quiet, but proud of my small/ huge achievement. I loved her so much in that moment and felt that sense of belonging I had always craved in my drinking days. She made me feel welcomed and that I fit in no matter how little I knew about the sport. Because of her kindness, I went back again.

Slowly, ok not so slowly, I became a part of the community. The men weren't so scary; they didn't even hit on me. I was an equal. My body started changing. I was getting strong and muscular and within two months, I signed up for full time and was going four to five days a week.

I gained weight, a good 15 pounds of meat. This made me feel safe — only a certain type of man would be able to handle a woman with muscle. A strong woman would attract a strong man, not the cowards from my past. I saw the women wearing little shorts with such confidence and the men not even batting an eye.

I bought a pair and wore them as a giant middle finger to my rapist!

I found that it was okay to be attractive, it didn't mean I was going to get raped again. It didn't make me bad or wrong or a slut. It was okay to wear what I wanted when I wanted. I stopped seeking permission.

I had found my voice again and I fell in love with myself. I earned my own trust back. It was like each time I picked up that bar I was making amends to Bri for not standing up for myself three years before and it still feels that way today, almost two years later.

My body is no longer something that needs to be punished, exploited or hidden. It is a machine and it works and I appreciate what it does and how it looks today. I am proud of it; it's more than just a receptacle for a man or some object to be used or abused...especially by me.

I learned to trust men again, besides the male coaches Dan and Jake and Sherpa. My first friend was Chad (yes, his name being Chad is not lost on me — ha!). He is warm and kind and he loves his wife. He was never leery or creepy or inappropriate. We joked and laughed and sweated and suffered together, and I felt safe for the first time being friendly with a man.

I found that I didn't want anything from these men either; they became my brothers, not conquests or saviors. Brothers. This was only the beginning.

As I got better and stronger and more comfortable in my skin, I started to compete and found that I was good at this thing. Not the best and not the worst — humility.

I was right sized for the first time. Dan pushed me to do more, to be better than I ever thought I could be. He showed me myself and held me accountable. He has been my greatest teacher (he is also my greatest frustration — ha!). Dan can be so pushy, but it's because he expects my best and I had never given my best before. I was the queen of quitting and mediocrity. He's very honest, blunt, or even harsh at times (I need it and respect him for that), and he has the biggest heart of anyone I know. He would do anything to help any one of us and I trust this man with my life.

Dan told me to never settle and to hold out for the best, and I listen to him because I value his opinion like that of my own dad and brother. I'll never be able to thank him for what he's given to me by creating this place for all of us to come together. The monthly dues seem so insignificant to what I get in return.

I met my soulmates here, my best friends, and I've been blessed with some of the most difficult people I've had to deal with (so many personalities). All of them gifts to me on this journey of self betterment. I'm constantly growing and learning and being shown more about Bri and who and what I want to be.

Never in my life have I been more challenged physically, mentally, and emotionally. I get to be of service and pass along what I have learned in and out of the box. I get to be a cheerleader and be cheered for, and I let them cheer for me. Today I can let people love me.

I've convinced most of my friends and family to come try this thing out and now the family that once had no choice but to drink in order to spend time with me are now fit and healthy and happy. We are present together.

I connect to people today on a level that terrified me before. I am open and honest, and I have learned about real integrity and accountability. It's amazing what happens to your relationships when you actually listen and share your truth with another human being without the presence of alcohol, when you get to remember every beautiful second.

CrossFit Spokane Valley is so much more than a gym. It is my home, one of my thinnest of spaces where I can connect to my source. Where my God speaks to me through the beautiful humans that I get to workout with. Pushing through and suffering together brings people closer. So does sharing each other's triumphs and victories, no matter how big or small.

We celebrate being alive and we connect to one another. My soul was healed here, I was reborn here, I am a Phoenix and I have risen from the ashes more beautiful than before.

A few months ago I saw Chad driving in his work truck. There was no fear or anger this time. I looked over at him and I forgave him. Then I wept tears of gratitude that I no longer had to hold that hate in my heart. I was free.

Story Thirty-One

Martin Veilleux

Je me suis toujours déplacé en fauteuil roulant...

Je suis Martin Veilleux, une personne handicapée né avec le Spina Bifida; une malformation congénitale de la moelle épinière. Devenu complètement non-voyant en 2007 à l'âge de 28 ans, dû à une hydrocéphalie diagnostiquée à la naissance, vous ne me verrez jamais sans mon chien. Il est pour moi mon guide, mon ami et mon protecteur. La Fondation Mira fournit des chiens d'assistance pour personne non-voyante ou handicapée.

Mon handicap ne m'a pas empêché de suivre les traces de mon père et j'ai travaillé aux services des comptes pour les banques TD et Royale. Durant l'année 2004, ma vue s'est dégradée du côté gauche. Je poursuivis tout de même mon chemin et mon travail alors au comptoir multi-services à la ville de Laval durant deux ans.

Dès mon plus jeune âge, le sport a fait partie intégrante de ma vie. De l'âge de 6 à 26 ans, j'ai joué au hockey sur luge comme gardien de but. De 2000 à 2004, j'ai fait parti de l'équipe canadienne en caressant le rêve d'aller aux Jeux Paralympiques de 2006. Malheureusement, devenu de moins en moins voyant, j'ai dû modifier mon parcours... et réapprendre à vivre complètement.
De nature combattante et avec l'aide de mes proches, de l'Institut Nazareth et Louis Braille, je me suis relevé les manches pour continuer à savourer ce que la vie m'offrait.

Un nouveau sport est alors entré dans ma vie. L'aviron a été pour moi une source de liberté et d'évasion. Ce rêve fut possible grâce à la collaboration du Club d'aviron de Laval et de l'Association québécoise d'aviron qui ont conçu une embarcation et des rames adaptées pour moi.

Durant l'été 2013, j'ai voulu relever de nouveaux défis. J'ai rencontré une personne qui m'a parlé de CrossFit et depuis, je m'y consacre à un rythme de quatre fois par semaine.

Ce sport m'apporte la possibilité de me dépasser. Avec l'aide des entraineurs de CrossFit Laval, tout ceci devient possible. Ceux-ci adaptent les exercices et les routines d'entrainement afin de me permettre de travailler autant que les autres membres du club.

La camaraderie et l'esprit de famille qui règne au sein des membres me permettent de me sentir comme tout le monde.
Je recommande ce sport merveilleux à tous ceux qui recherchent un dépassement, de l'adrénaline et des émotions fortes.

Depuis que je suis non-voyant, j'ai dû aussi modifier ma carrière. Je donne maintenant des conférences dans les écoles et les entreprises pour livrer mon message de motivation, de détermination et de persévérance.
Je terminerai en citant Victor Hugo : « Quand l'œil du corps s'éteint; l'œil de l'esprit s'allume » Dans la vie, chaque obstacle est contournable. Avec la ferme volonté d'obtenir l'ultime succès; tout rêve devient possible.

***

I always moved in a wheelchair...

I'm Martin Veilleux, a disabled person born with Spina Bifida, a congenital malformation of the spinal cord. I became totally blind in 2007 at the age of 28, due to hydrocephalus, which was also diagnosed at birth. You will never see me without my dog. For me, he is my guide, my friend and my protector. I was fortunate enough to be given this dog through The Mira Foundation, which provides assistance dogs for blind or disabled people.

My disability did not stop me from following my father's footsteps, as I've worked in Account Services at the TD and Royal banks. During 2004, my eyesight deteriorated but I still continued my way and my work in the multi-service counter at the City of Laval for the next two years.

From an early age, sport has been an integral part of my life. From the age of 6 to 26 years old, I played sledge hockey as a goalkeeper. From 2000 to 2004, I was a member of the Canadian team, caressing the dream of going to the Paralympic Games in 2006. Unfortunately, as I became more and more sightless, I had to modify my route...and learn to live fully but also differently.

Born with a fighting nature and with the help of my family and the Nazareth & Louis Braille Institute, I rolled up my sleeves to continue to enjoy what life has to offer.

Then, a new sport entered my life. For four years, rowing has been for me a source of freedom and escape. This dream has been made possible through the collaboration of the Laval Rowing Club and the Quebec Rowing Association, who designed a boat and oars adapted to my needs.

In the summer of 2013, I felt the need for additional challenges. I met a person who told me about CrossFit and since then I have devoted myself to this training regime four times per week.

This sport is giving me the opportunity to exceed what I thought were my limits. With the help of the CrossFit Laval coaches, all this is becoming possible. They are adapting the exercises and workout routines to allow me to train as much as the other members of the club.

The camaraderie and family spirit that reigns within this box allows me to feel like everyone else.

I recommend this wonderful sport to anyone looking for an overflow of adrenaline and strong emotions.

Since I am blind, I also had to change my career. I am now giving talks and conferences to schools and businesses in order to deliver my message of motivation, determination, and perseverance.

I will conclude by quoting Victor Hugo: *"When the eye of the body goes out, the eye of the spirit ignites."*

In life, every obstacle can be overcome. With the firm determination to get the ultimate success, any dream is possible.

Story Thirty-Two

Stephanie Peter

I was like many others. I came from a dance background, then started working out after a horrible breakup with a boyfriend who I thought was "the one." I did a few duathlons, dabbled in some martial arts...and then I found CrossFit. For a while I felt invincible juggling it all, but after some time, excitement grew throughout the box and before I knew it, I was refreshing my phone every Thursday night in anticipation of the next 2012 Open workout. I began to focus all of my energy into one thing: CrossFit.

I was addicted to the feeling of having teammates and strangers interested in my performance, surrounding me as I moved through each rep. I loved how powerful it felt to use God's gifts to me to their greatest potential, being among the best in the city and knowing I could keep up with them. It was clear — I loved the element of competition and it was an honour to represent my box at Regionals that year. I felt like I was on cloud nine; it was just like I had seen in all the videos on YouTube, and it was all becoming a reality.

I would sign up for absolutely everything to keep testing my limits, and after Regionals that year, a new competition came on to the scene and, of course, I wanted in on the action. It was the Sweat RX Championships and, similar to Regionals, you had to qualify by submitting three different scores for three different workouts.

It was the end of May and geez, it was starting to get hot in the box. I moved through the first workout one Saturday morning, which involved a row, some overhead squats, and later on that week a teammate and I did the second workout, heavy deadlifts and chest to bar pull ups.

I felt confident about this one. I pushed myself beyond my expectations. I hopped up to the bar for my last set of chest to bars and decided not to chalk, because there was simply no time for that. I hit my first rep great, but there was no strength left in my forearms. My brain was telling me to keep going.

My body gave out and I fell flat on my back with a

loud smack. I instantly knew something was not right. I lay there for a second and tried to assess just how serious the damage was. My coach helped me off the ground, and I hobbled to the car.

Here began a series of visits to the emergency ward. After hours of waiting, that feeling you get when you are in the middle of a WOD and in "the suck" started to seep in, but I was able to stay positive. Let's just say CrossFit does more than make you better at exercising; it teaches you lessons of how to pull through in the worst of situations. It was then, in that moment, that I felt these lessons come together, that I really understood why CrossFit was put in my life.

Within weeks, I was back on my feet, doing what gave me a reason to live. It was competition day for the Sweat RX Championships, and although I still had some remnants of a pinched nerve from the fall, I was going to give it my best shot.

The day started with a shorter couplet of toes to bar and kettlebell swings. Toes to bar was not my forte. In fact, I finished dead last, but I didn't care. The barbell complex was next, and now it was my time to shine. I had practiced this at the box and felt really confident that this one would put me ahead. I progressed in weight to build up to my best effort. I did it! I hit the weight I had practiced and I was feeling fantastic.

Little time remained on the clock, and in the true spirit of CrossFit, I loaded it up and marched into the unknown. This weight was uncharted territory for me but with the crowd behind me, I was going to give it a go. With 10 seconds left, I took the first snatch. I threw it hard. I caught it at the bottom, but with a loud "smack" I hit the ground. There was an audible "pop" simultaneous to the sound of a human body hitting the ground.

I laid there, trying to make the same assessment I had made the first time I had hit the ground. As much as I didn't want to admit it, I knew it was bad. After a few minutes lying there motionless, I tried to get up. Success! Now I tried to walk; my knee was stiff and had started to swell, but again, another success. It was more of a hobble than a walk, but one foot at a time I did it.

This was the start of a two year process. Six months later, the MRI determined I had a torn ACL and meniscus.

There is such beauty in CrossFit, because even with someone in my condition, there was still lots I could do at the box. The support of the community was paramount and I wasn't going to let a knee injury stand in my way of having them by my side.

I still went in and trained five days a week, but when the barbell is your safe haven, having a knee injury lets the dust build up on your lifting shoes. The surgery was a huge success. In fact, this whole event in my life was a huge success. It made me realize that sometimes you really do need to take one step back before you leap and bound forward.

This setback not only made my will stronger, but also physically helped me achieve things I never thought possible. It was through this challenge that I was forced to work the gymnastics movements I dreaded. Movements like handstand push-ups and muscle ups were merely just a dream, and they have now become a reality and a strength because of the "waist up" training I did throughout the recovery process.

During this time, I forgot what it felt like to hold a barbell in my hands. Looking to make sure I would bounce back on the right path, I was set up with one of the best weightlifting coaches in the city, and he made me realize my love for the barbell once again. Step by step, he helped me get back on my feet. Not only did he help me through recovery, he helped me to provincial and national level ranks.

It seems crazy, but I'm so grateful for this whole experience. I have met amazing new people and reached goals I thought were merely dreams.

Story Thirty-Three

Jeynelle Broatch

Friday, March 1, 2013, I was diagnosed with breast cancer. At the time I was on maternity leave from my job, looking after our seven month old son. As you can well imagine, the news was shocking but practicality had to take over and that's exactly what happened in my life and that included my training.

I had started CrossFit about two years earlier when my trainer, Kath, opened *CrossFit Richmond* with her husband, Adam. I'd trained with Kath elsewhere for the three years prior and figured I'd give it a go for a month and, like many others, I've never looked back.

During my pregnancy I had kept training right up to delivery. Having this recent experience with scaling, I had no intention to stop training through cancer treatment either. So after the initial teary discussion with Kath and Adam, it was back to business with some scaling as needed.

The first chemo regime was the tough stuff, four rounds in three weekly cycles. Chemo didn't "hurt" but practically knocked me out of life in the week that followed. I could no longer look after our baby in week one of the cycle nor could I train that week. But, in the two "good" weeks of each cycle, I could manage both.

Cancer requires many doctors' appointments and timing these with baby sleep times is difficult, but the trainers helped me out immensely. I could drop into the box whenever someone was there, not needing to wait for a session time.

Two weeks in and I experienced my first hiccup. After training one Sunday morning and feeling generally fine, I became extremely tired later that afternoon. Dismissing it as the effects of chemo, I took myself off to bed. By early the next morning, fever had set in and we were on our way to the emergency department. At first I thought I would just need some IV antibiotics and then be sent home, but the blood tests revealed the chemo had wiped out my white blood cells and I had picked up a systemic infection. I had to be admitted for a few days.

This was the first night I had ever spent away from our baby.

Even having worked as a health professional myself for many years and treating hundreds of patients, I had no idea or respect for how much people have to keep changing expectations when they are seriously unwell. My plans for one week off and two weeks on were again paired back. This meant training, yes, but no pushing my body to exhaustion.

At first I found this contrary to the CrossFit ethos and

I battled with this concept of not totally pushing myself. Eventually I figured it out and preferred to think of it as maintaining control and listening to my body.

The next six months of chemo were a blurry cycle of doctor's appointments, blood tests, and treatments. I continued to train over this period for a dose of "normal life." I was still able to achieve goals, even getting my first muscle up during this time, but nothing that totally exhausted me. I needed to be around strong-minded, strong people, and even my friends who were not CrossFitters, made sure I could train to keep my sanity and remain positive.

The next phase was getting through my surgery — a right mastectomy and removal of all the lymph nodes in my right arm. Again, I had no idea of the impact this would have physically on my body, namely on my shoulder. My right shoulder was seriously tight from "cording" and scar tissue. I also had a tissue expander, which I fondly referred to as the "rock," which had been put in place to prevent my external skin from shrinking during the upcoming radiation.

Seven weeks and four days after surgery (not that I was counting!), I was back in the gym.

"Excited" doesn't explain the satisfaction of returning after such a surgery. My first session was 1:1 with Kath and she kept an extra close eye on me, knowing well that I was super keen — probably a little too keen! We went through just six movements for shoulder mobility. I didn't feel strong physically but satisfied with just being in the building.

Around this time, a friend referred me to a skilled physio who specialized in post mastectomy rehab. I was seeing her twice per week to try and get rid of my dreadful cording, and training 1:1 sessions with Kath. Trying to massage the cording out of my armpit was painful and in the words of my therapist, "physio terrorism." But the pain was over in a few minutes and I likened it to a nasty Tabata session.

I'm pleased to say it was all worth it. Kath took weekly photos of my shoulder range and it was encouraging to see the progress. At exactly eight weeks and four days post mastectomy, I completed my first WOD, a five minute AMRAP of double unders, GHD sit ups, and Russian kettlebell swings. I had almost forgotten how much fun it is to do WODs!

A few weeks passed and then I entered the final stage of treatment: two months of radiation therapy. At first I had no issues and could continue to train, but after three weeks of treatment the radiation burn set in and my skin had become too delicate for training. I couldn't risk raising a sweat, much less hold a bar in the rack position. So it was another training break and this time an opportunity to think about the year ahead.

This mainly meant fantasizing about returning to my

former level of fitness, but I did one constructive thing and signed up for my level one trainer's course, which made me feel like I was still involved. I dragged myself through the remaining weeks of radiation and eventually the final day came. I practically jumped off the table and ran out of the place. The radiation was by far the longest "chipper" I had ever done.

Finally, in May 2014, I received the phone call from my doctor to confirm I was clear from cancer. The months that followed were a blur of relief and normal life activities that our family had been denied in the year prior. I was somewhere between excited and exhausted and I didn't quite know what to do with myself.

Training throughout this experience never felt like something I "chose" but was the right thing for me to do.

Being around strong-minded, strong people had a profound effect on my ability to cope with the experience mentally and physically. None of this was achieved alone but with the un-quivering support of my husband, our families, in particular my mother and mother-in-law, who looked after our little family in the "sick" times, my close friends who cooked meals and cared for my son to allow me time to go to the gym and, of course, our solid community from *CrossFit Richmond* who always had the doors open for me.

Today, I enjoy my workouts without any serious movement restrictions. I am conscious of proper warm up and listen to my body closely for signals that it has had enough, particularly in my right shoulder area. Overhead movements are my biggest weakness.

My goal is to gain enough confidence in my fitness to participate in a masters competition in August 2015. I have earned my CrossFit Kids certification and enjoy coaching new mothers. Together, we appreciate this precious time spent on fitness and enjoy the positivity and motivation generated when we gather.

Story Thirty-Four

Jessica Poissant

"Hello, my name is [...] and I'm going to help you; what's your name?"

This is something you learn to say in CPR classes when faced with people in distress. Someone said those exact words to me on June 4, 2013, just after I was unpinned from beneath the car that had just hit me. Never have I felt so much pain at once, but somehow in the ambulance ride to the hospital I thought, *"It's probably not so bad; I'll be back at the gym in a few weeks. This sucks, I really liked the training I was going to do today. "*

I have no idea how much time passed from the moment I got hit to the moment I was admitted to intensive care, but it felt like forever.

Once the adrenaline settled down and I really started to feel all my broken bones and my open wounds, I could not stop crying — from pain, but also from fear. In less than a few hours, my boyfriend, my closest friend, and my family were by my side. I spent the next nine days at the hospital.

My two brothers, my parents, my sister, and my in-laws took shifts staying with me. I was never alone and for this I will forever be grateful because I could not do anything by myself. I was not even able to push the button to call a nurse.

My boyfriend, Louis-Pierre, and I had opened our box, *CrossFit Rosemont,* just eight months before this event. We had a business that needed all of our attention. Before I had time to worry about it, friends and coaches from other boxes in Montreal, who learned about my accident, had already stepped up to help us cover my coaching hours. Friends came to visit me at the hospital. Gym members sent me flowers and cards with wonderful words of support.

My injuries were not life threatening, but I had many. I had multiple fractures in my left arm, I had broken fingers in my right hand, and my middle finger was completely opened. I had a broken leg, a twisted ankle, and multiple road burns on my face and hands. I underwent two reconstructive surgeries while hospitalized (one for my left forearm, the second for my right middle finger).

After I was released from the hospital, I knew the hard part was ahead of me.

I moved in with my in-laws for the next month. I needed help to get around, and I could not eat, shower, or go to the bathroom by myself. Because of this accident, my boyfriend, Louis-Pierre, was alone to take care of our gym. He took care of everything relating to the business all by himself in order for me to be able to recover. It is not easy for a grown, independent adult to have to be taken care of like this. It took a huge effort in letting go.

My road to recovery was challenging. What kept me going, even during hard times, was the support I received from my loved ones, my friends, and my gym members. Every day I had small victories, from trying to get dressed to brushing my teeth and putting cream on my face. Every little thing was a milestone.

Within a month I was back home and moving, slowly, once again in the gym. Mostly on the stationary bike.

During the summer I started occupational therapy and physiotherapy. I spent countless hours doing simple exercises to get my hands to heal properly. I did OT for almost a year and still do physio once in a while for pain that is not entirely gone. My therapists (they CrossFit now!) played a huge part in my recovery.

Five months after the accident, in October, I needed to go for a third surgery — a bone graft for a fracture that would not heal in my left arm. Before my third surgery was complete, I could not really train. I could not put any weights on my left arm, even transporting groceries from the store to home (500m) was out of the question.

I had so many mobility issues from not really moving

in the past months and from the damage my body went through that I knew I could not plan my rehab by myself. During the fall of 2013, I sought help and started working with Karim and *Rx Lab.*

Trying to build my fitness back up was very challenging. Every day is a fight. Everything is hard, especially when you remember how well and easily you could do things before. My coach really emphasized the importance of what I could do NOW, the baby steps that would lead me back to health instead of comparing with what I could do before.

I worked hard to think that way and celebrate every small victory. My first weeks of training were mainly muscle activation and mobility. Finally, on January 28, 2014, my orthopedic surgeon told me I was ready to go. My arm showed great improvement and I could start lifting weights again. That meant I could also go back to coaching again.

I still had a lot of work to do in order to get back to where I was. It took a long time before I was able to overhead squat or hold a pull-up bar without suffering intolerable pain. It took a lot of baby steps; however, I was rewarded with huge improvements over the course of a year.

Every day when I step foot in the gym, I am amazed at what I can do despite all my injuries. This accident helped me learn to let go of what I could not control and taught me to trust the process. Now, when I have a bad training day, I stop being angry at myself and just accept it for what it is: a bad day.

The idea of being able to train again is what has kept me going during the full year of rehab. I pushed through the pain and the discouragement, and I am happy I did. I am also very grateful for the wonderful community at my gym and the support of my coach. I could not have made it without these amazing and understanding people surrounding me.

In 2015, I completed my first OPEN since the accident.

My goal was to have fun and do one WOD RX. I ended doing four out of five RX and had tons of fun. I enjoyed every moment of it, and I finished 1039th in Canada East, which I think is pretty awesome. These OPEN WODs were very emotional, especially the chest-to-bar and overhead squat workout, because at one point I did not know if I would ever be able to do these two movements again. I cried at the end of the workout because I realized I had really made it. I could say the accident was truly behind me.

While my rehab is "officially" over, the story does not end there. I will continue to work hard. I am planning on competing in CrossFit and weightlifting during the summer of 2015 and pushing myself even further. If I can survive a collision with 1000 pounds of metal, nothing can stop me now.

*****

Jessica Poissant is the co-owner of CrossFit Rosemont in Montreal. Her rehab was made possible by Rx Lab.

Story Thirty-Five

Jenny Elsaesser

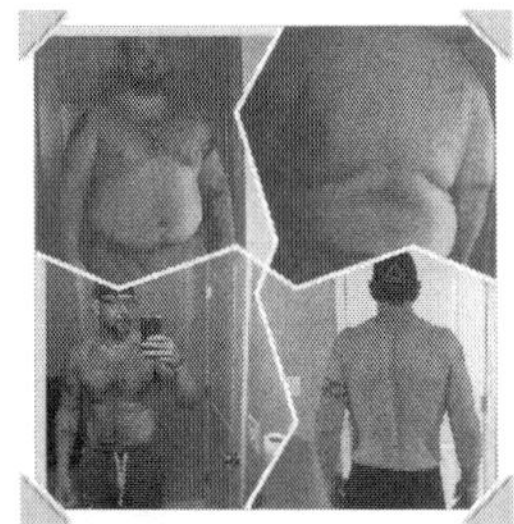

My story is boring — well not boring, just typical. I'll sum it up briefly: "Hi, my name is Jenny, and CrossFit changed my life."

I was a woman facing middle age, struggling with my body and not knowing how to change. I heard about a new CrossFit box and walked in and my life changed. It helped me see my worth, encouraged me to dig deep and never quit, and became to me a community of amazing people that helped me overcome my fears and discover the hidden me, and emerge even stronger, even more confident...

This is the story for many people. And it's a great story.

But I want to tell the story of the person who made it

possible for me and many others to experience such success — Coach J.

You can find Coach Jeremy Johnston most days at his box, *CrossFit Sevier,* and if you happen to stop by while he's working out, you will most likely hear music with motivational speakers in the background. Like Sylvester Stallone's quote as Rocky, *"Life's not about how hard of a hit you can give...it's about how many you can take and still keep moving forward."* More music...then a quote from Will Smith's character in The Pursuit of Happiness: *"You got a dream...You gotta protect it. People can't do somethin' themselves, they wanna tell you you can't do it. If you want somethin', go get it. Period."* And the music plays on with more and more quotes.

And there Coach J will be giving 100% to some torturous WOD he's concocted for himself, a WOD that is different from what he's programmed for the rest of us since he's limited on what he can do — right now — because of an ongoing injury he was dealt years ago.

In high school, Coach J was that big fit kid that played football and wrestled.

After graduation, he felt the calling to do something more with his life. So he enlisted in the Navy and served for about eight years until a life changing event occurred. While serving in Iraq during 9/11, he went on leave, November 7, 2001, to visit his grandparents.

After picking him up at the airport, their car was hit head on by a drunk driver. His grandmother was killed and his grandfather was critically injured and would later succumb to his injuries. His two year old daughter was miraculously and thankfully unharmed.

Jeremy was sitting in the backseat and fractured his neck, had broken ribs, a broken ankle, and also suffered a shattered femur, pelvis and hip. But he survived. Doctors told him that he would never walk without assistance again.

After numerous surgeries to repair his leg, pelvis, and hip, he worked hard through physical therapy to regain some measure of mobility. However, this injury left him with chronic pain that lead to depression, inactivity, and eventual obesity. Over a period of eleven years he gained over 120 pounds, weighing a total of 360 pounds.

"Don't cry to quit! You already in pain, you already hurt! Get a reward from it!" ~ Eric Thomas

After numerous efforts by his family to get Jeremy some help, his mom finally encouraged him to try out a place she'd heard about. He listened and found the courage to walk into *Five Rivers CrossFit* in Morristown, Tennessee. The amazing coaches there motivated him and helped him fight through his fear, his weight, his pain and feelings of inadequacy.

Their encouragement and coaching helped him to lose over 140 pounds in a year and a half. He gained back his confidence and his fitness. The man who was never supposed to walk unassisted again, not only was walking, but was running, squatting, lifting weights...

"If you can imagine it, you can achieve it; if you can dream it, you can become it." ~ William Arthur Ward

In 2013, Jeremy Johnston became 'Coach J' and opened his own box, *CrossFit Sevier*, in Sevierville, Tennessee. His mother, Pam, his father, Reg, and his brother, Jason, all played a part in helping Jeremy achieve his dream. *CrossFit Sevier* became Jeremy's passion, and he has been able to pass on all that his life has taught him and enable others to dig deep and find their better selves.

I entered this story at the opening of *CrossFit Sevier*. I was one of the original members. I, and many others were the first to be inspired by his dedication, passion, and commitment to fitness, health, and living life.

"When the messenger of misery visits you, what are you going to do? What will keep you in the game?" ~ Les Brown

And in the midst of all these successes, life continued to happen. Just slightly over a year into his endeavors, Coach J was experiencing serious pain in his hip. A trip to the VA uncovered that the hardware holding his hip had become insecure. He had another surgery to take out the screws. It was then a waiting game to see how his hip would continue without the hardware.

Then in August, 2014, his mother Pam was diagnosed with Stage 4 colon cancer. Since then, she has been fighting through chemotherapy and other treatments. His father, Reg, in order to keep the insurance that pays for these treatments, has had to keep working at a job out of state.

I kept a watchful eye on Jeremy, expecting everything to crash since his support system was being attacked from all sides. But he didn't quit, and with the help of his brother — who also has his Level 1 — and other members, he has coached through it all.

More recently, at the beginning of 2015, continuing pain in Coach J's hip forced him to limit his activities while undergoing physical therapy to try to turn the muscles around his hip into a better position before determining whether he would need hip replacement. Although this news might sound disheartening, it hasn't kept Coach J down one bit. He continues to show us all that you can fight through anything and still achieve your goals. That in the midst of pain and hardship, you don't quit, you just find different ways to fight.

Yes, my story is a little humdrum compared to his. But he also taught me that we are all fighting our own battles, and just because they are different doesn't make them any less significant.

So my story, his story, your story...they are not boring.

I know I could have written a story about me and my transformation, and you would have been inspired. But Coach J's story needed to be told, and my story is part of his. It is his continuing story and many others like his that make our stories possible. If you asked him he'd tell you his story; in fact, he enjoys speaking at functions to help motivate others. But Jeremy is not the kind to pat himself on the back and advertise it, so I will.

CrossFit is a thriving community because of people like Coach J. He was inspired and motivated by someone to become someone who inspires and motivates people like me...who hopes to inspire and motivate people...

I think my story is just beginning.

*****

Coach Jeremy Johnston continues to coach at CrossFit Sevier. He most recently earned his Level 2 Advanced Sports Performance Coaching Certification from ETSU USA Weightlifting. His mom, Pam, is still fighting cancer.

Jennifer Elsaesser is still training at CrossFit Sevier and is continually working on her story.

Story Thirty-Six

Raynique Ducie and Jonathan Ducie

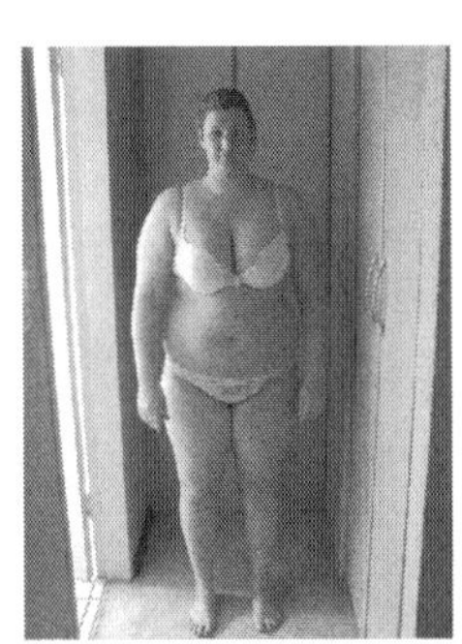

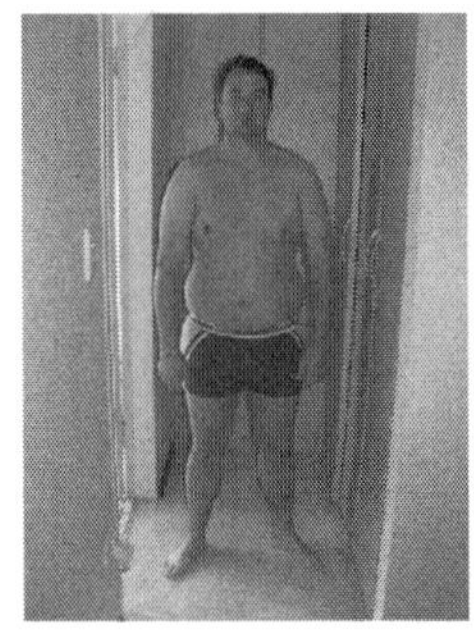

When I met my husband, Jonathan Ducie, in my early twenties, I was (somewhat) health conscious, felt good about myself, and led an active lifestyle. He played rugby at club level and maintained a good body weight.

Somehow, somewhere, and perhaps due to multiple personal tragedies that affected us both, we lost sight of what it meant to be healthy.

We drank too much, followed by a "what I want, when I want it" eating plan, and slowly but surely stopped all physical activity. We married four years later and we each weighed about 20kgs more than when we had met. After our wedding day, we fell into the dreaded "comfort zone," with continued weight gain and unhealthy living.

Sure, we tried to get to the gym a few times a week and believed that that was enough. We lived in denial about how we looked and the damage we were doing to our bodies. Looking at photographs of ourselves from this period is a stark reminder of just how out of shape and unhealthy we truly were. In retrospect, all we can think is: *"How, how did we let ourselves get to that point?"*

I do remember feeling shy, worthless and ugly, not wanting to leave the house or socialize. Our daily routine revolved around TV and mealtimes, instant gratification, and laziness. How I felt about myself certainly affected my marriage, as I lacked the confidence to enjoy my marriage fully.

Realizing where we were headed, a family member suggested that we try this new type of gym called "CrossFit." I was skeptical. I liked lazing on the couch in front of the TV and doing nothing all weekend. I liked the anonymity of going to a big gym where no one knew my name.

Reluctantly, I tried it. I arrived for an "Introduction to CrossFit" class at *360Vida* in my long, bulky tracksuit pants, old takkies, and oversized t-shirt, and hated every minute. My husband, on the other hand, was instantly hooked. He pushed me to keep going, even though it really didn't feel like it was getting any easier.

I remember being absolutely mortified as my coaches, William and Diane, tried to flip my hefty body over to teach me the movement for a "skin the cat." I'm pretty sure Di got a knee to the face and Will pulled a bicep trying to get me top-over-tail. A few months in, Will looked at my red, frustrated, angry face after a WOD and asked me, *"Are you ever going to look like you enjoy CrossFit?"*

That was three years ago. Now — I honestly couldn't live without it.

Between the two of us, my husband and I have lost more than 60kgs (also known as an entire medium-sized adult). Yes, we got all the usual benefits that a dedicated exercise and healthy eating regime would give you: weight loss, muscle gain, body confidence, good health, etc., but with that we also got plugged into a community that is fun, supportive, and active.

We have made lifelong friends and we can't stand lying about all weekend. We have a renewed passion for life, for each other, for our marriage; it's much easier to treat your partner with respect when you respect yourself.

Apart from marital bliss, in many ways, CrossFit has also taught me how to deal better with stress and, as I run my own company, it has taught me how to handle a large workload.

Need to proofread a 220 page document? No problem, it's a 10 Round-For-Time WOD with 22 reps in each round. I've developed greater stamina and a dedication to seeing things through, even when my body (or my mind) wants to quit.

We may not be where we want to be yet, we may still have a long way to go, but we are progressing towards our goals in a healthy way, supporting each other as we go.

This journey to health never ends; it must be a lifelong focus with milestones and goals set along the way. To us, CrossFit and the healthy living it promotes has become a way of life, an ethos, something we will pass on to our children, our family, our friends — to anyone that wants to improve themselves.

Story Thirty-Seven

James Mallia

It was another chilly October Saturday morning in Albany, New York, as I was waking up to get ready for the big day. In my junior year of high school I had finally made the cross country varsity team. I woke up with excitement and some nervousness and I proceeded with my morning rituals. Today would be my first varsity race!

As I took a sip from a freshly poured cup of coffee, I caught myself against the kitchen counter. I stated loudly "that's weird" as my mother looked over with concern. My heart started to pound. My mother asked, *"What happened?"* In confusion, I replied, *"I don't know. The entire left side of my body just fell asleep."* I could see the fear in my mother's eyes as she told me to lay down on the floor.

My mother proceeded to call 911 as I begged her not to, scared that the situation was serious and I just wanted to try and fight through it. She quickly convinced me to get down as the pain sank in and my screams that sounded like murder filled the house. I used my only working hand and held my head, rolling side to side in agony until I blacked out.

I was rushed to the hospital where they discovered I had suffered a massive brain hemorrhage from a ruptured brain aneurysm. The cause was from a rare genetic birth defect known as an arteriovenous malformation. I was quickly placed in a medically induced coma to relieve the swelling in my brain. The doctors came to visit my mother for the first time, with faces of fear. How does one tell a mother that her 16 year old son could die?

They told her to make a phone call to my father, who lived in Long Island, New York.

I would later go in for successful procedures to plug up the aneurysm. Following two weeks of surgeries and recovery, I began to wake up from the induced coma. I was slowly made aware of what had taken place. This was a difficult time because I just didn't fully understand, and added to that, being heavily medicated made everything seem like a blur.

I remember waking up one night and while looking at my mother in a panic, saying, *"we have to go or we will be late!"* In confusion she asked me, *" To where?"* I replied, *"I have to race!"* My mind was always wanting to compete.

The desire to fight, and now fight for my life, was just in my nature.

After being in the hospital for three weeks I was transferred to a rehabilitation center. During this time the doctors didn't know what functions I had lost and what I would ever gain back. My determination to regain as much as possible, to return to normalcy, never wavered. I knew the only way to beat this was to stay focused on what I needed to do, and not to feel self pity.

I said to myself, *"What happened has happened and it can't be changed. I can only control my future."* This started my long journey toward a new and different life. I had to relearn my first walking steps but not before I learned how to crawl. Although this process was painful, I never let the struggles get in my way. When I was asked to rest while taking my first steps, I refused, as I had a runner's mentality to keep moving and pushing forward.

I began walking again in less than two months post aneurysm. This amazing accomplishment was only the first step. I continued to make many gains in my rehabilitation and was released to "outpatient" care around Thanksgiving. Following my release and continued outpatient care, I was looking forward to catching up with my school studies. Another goal I had set for myself was to catch up on missed work, and to graduate on time.

Not only did I return to school, I felt like I also returned to my "family." I had developed close relationships during the years of being a part of the indoor and outdoor cross country teams. My teammates had become much like family to me, and spending time with them gave me a sense of normalcy.

I ran my first three mile race the following fall. Even though I knew I would finish last every single race, it didn't matter. I loved to run and be around my team and this became my focus. Finishing the races became my goal. After graduation, I lost the thing that I loved and my motivation to keep going.

Once in college, I didn't have the support I needed to continue to race and be part of a team. I tried going to the gym on and off multiple times but was never consistent simply because it was just not the same. That team and family aspect was missing.

It wouldn't be until almost five years later that I was able to replace that support system. My cousin, Michael, knew I had recently moved to Long Island in New York and that I was interested in going to a gym. I had never heard of CrossFit but he explained to me that it's something I might enjoy and a good way to meet new people.

I was nervous to begin because of my condition and the adaptive process. The owner of *CrossFit Rapture*, along with the other coaches, taught me how the dynamics of CrossFit were much different than a regular gym. I instantly fell in love with it. CrossFit was something totally new and it restarted a lost drive that I hadn't had since high school.

The competitive nature of CrossFit was a perfect match for my personality. Despite my limitations, I continued to improve my overall fitness level. Fitness wasn't the only thing I gained. I quickly learned that the gym worked as a team to help each member through workouts.

I had at long last found the family that I was missing all these years, a community that supports each other and has fun along the way.

I was given the opportunity to compete in the Working Wounded Games and it was eye opening. A level playing field amongst adaptive athletes was incredible.

CrossFit has not only benefited me as a competitive athlete, but in other areas of my life as well. I gained the confidence to go back to college and work toward a Master's program. CrossFit has allowed me to regain my focus and become a more clear-minded, driven person. I am constantly achieving goals that I would never have thought I could.

It is because of CrossFit that I am continuing a path of success and healing all types of wounds in my life.

****

James continues to train in CrossFit and competes each year in the Working Wounded Games held in Virginia. He is pursuing his degree in Psychology, with plans to enter the Master's program.

Story Thirty-Eight

Caroline Nairn

I turned 50 years old in December 2014 and it was that event looming over me that convinced me to try CrossFit.

I was diagnosed with Type 1 diabetes at age six, and encouraged by all the doctors I saw to engage in sport. So, I did. From the age of 12, I competed in field hockey, lacrosse, and basketball for three hours every afternoon after school, depending on the season. My best friend and I did extra training on the weekends.

The pressure from my family has always been to be the best at everything, to win, to beat everyone else, and I tried to do just that with more and more training. Diabetes was proof that my body wasn't perfect and I was ashamed of and embarrassed by the disease, so I did my best to deny it.

Then I went off to University. I lived in the center of a large city and I ran three to four times a week. Some days were definitely better than others, but mostly what I found challenging was exercising alone. It takes courage to face a long, repetitive workout day in and day out and maintain enthusiasm for it.

My University was very unusual in that one requirement was that we had to live in two cultures other than our own.

So, off to Kenya I went! I lived way out in the countryside, and culturally it was quite a shock. That I wanted to run, for fun, was seen as very weird. The villagers knew I ran at 5pm every afternoon, so they'd gather to watch me run home. It was like finishing a long race every day, with spectators. I used to come to the end of the road, whispering to myself "*the crowd is gathered around, watching Cary finish this epic run. She's looking great at this late stage!*"

This was all going well, until one day I was out running on a small footpath when a King Cobra, who'd been snoozing there, suddenly sat up about three feet in front of me and spread out his hood. I was so frightened, I simply froze. This was, accidentally, the right thing to do. We stared at each other for a bit — it seemed like an eternity! Eventually, the snake got bored and slid off into the grass. Once I stopped shaking, I sprinted for home!

Then I moved to London and joined a gym and did every aerobics class, going to about 10 classes per week, trying to live up to that 'perfect ideal' again. After three months I was getting bored, and didn't really feel all that fit. So I tried weight lifting, which I liked, but I was bored quickly again.

Then one day while I was struggling on a gym machine, one of the coaches said she thought I'd be good at triathlon. She helped me devise a training programme and I completed my first race about six months later.

As I took up triathlon, however, my marriage was becoming increasingly unhappy. I did what I'd done as a child and avoided going home by staying out longer and longer to train. I felt like I was in tip top shape.

Managing my Type 1 diabetes became a challenge. Long, slow aerobic training uses up blood sugar and the battle becomes about how to keep it sufficiently high enough.

The diabetes is just another thing I've had to manage and be aware of, especially during my sports activities. Mostly I've resented it, because it means that no matter how good I am, I can never achieve that ideal my parents gave me. The disease is always there, and you've always got to be aware of what is happening. I sometimes feel like I spend my life carting insulin, blood testing gear, and sugary snacks and drinks around.

I am angry at my body for being ill.

My first marriage ended, and to help myself with sadness over that, I began running again. But I'd make a commitment, get going for a few days, and then quit. A few weeks later, I'd do the same again. And again.

I took up smoking (not the wisest decision of my life), which didn't help things. This situation persisted for about eight years. I'd never been so inactive in my life.

However, other areas of my life saw improvement. I met my second husband, and we were having fun, eating out lots and drinking too much. I was gaining weight and feeling like crap.

In late 2014, with my 50th birthday approaching and feeling pretty dismal, but having quit smoking, I saw a Facebook post by a friend. She was moaning about how sore she was from her CrossFit intro. What?! That sounds really interesting!

I've come to regard this attitude as typical of CrossFit. *"What, you're aching all over because of a monster workout you did? I've got to try that!"* I'm not the only one who thinks this way, but other friends do regard me as slightly crazy.

I turned up for a taster session at *CrossFit Iron Duke*, woefully unfit and extremely nervous. My coach was

Toby, who carefully explained a lot of CrossFit ideas and put me through a brief workout. I was embarrassed about how little I could do (light years away from being better than everyone else), and Toby just scaled the necessary movements for me.

The bug had bitten. I signed up immediately for the six class intro course. Here was something interesting, that changed all the time, that I didn't have to do alone and that had lots of new things in it I'd never seen before. Who needs to learn how to do a double unders for triathlon training? Why would you want to be able to do a handstand if you're running?

I completed my full intro course and was photographed clutching my passing out certificate — which still hangs on the cork board in my study.

The time had come to join the regular classes with the cool kids. Nervous? No, terrified! I discussed it four times with one of the coaches at the gym, Kerry. That was three discussions more than was strictly necessary and Kerry will never get that time back.

Then one day, November 1st (a day that will live in infamy), I did it, and I've never looked back.

The interesting thing is not how much my fitness has improved — that could reasonably have been predicted. What is interesting is how much I've changed.

I have spent my life not telling anyone that I was diabetic because I was so ashamed about it, the physical evidence that I'd never be good enough. I wish I didn't have it, but I can now tell everyone that I do. Because the CrossFit approach of brief, intense exercise is completely different to long, slow repetitive training, instead of going down, my blood sugar shoots up in a workout.

To manage that, I have to have an injection of insulin between the warmup and the workout. There usually isn't a lot of time between the warmup and the workout, so I have my insulin with me and I inject in front of the other members of the class. It takes all of about five seconds, but until I joined CrossFit, I had never injected in front of anyone who didn't know me very well, and I never did it publicly.

Another thing I did was ask if I could have space in the refrigerator at the box to keep a Lucozade — sugar for if my blood sugar is getting too low. Managing diabetes is like walking a tightrope; you need to be in the middle all the time. If you stray too far to one side or the other (blood sugar too high or low), you need to make adjustments, fast.

Sometimes when I take the insulin prior to the workout, I take too much — it's an inexact science. That Lucozade in the fridge at the box is a public admission that I am diabetic. I did need it one day, but instead of making a false excuse and sneaking off into the changing room to chug one, I just left the workout, sprinted to the fridge and drank it down, sitting right there in the gym where everyone could see me. I couldn't rejoin the workout because I had to get my blood sugar back into a normal range and by the time I did, the workout was over. But, no one made a big deal out of it.

I think they didn't even notice apart from the coach that day who asked if I was okay. I didn't finish the workout, but I hit a PR: Through my actions I told everyone I am diabetic. It makes me quite tearful now, writing this, to think about how much I have hated myself, and the hell I have sometimes put myself through, over this damned disease.

The relief I feel to be able to write that last sentence is staggering, and it was CrossFit that helped me get there.

Because I am now 50, my body just can't do what it used to be able to do. When we have a really tough workout, I get pretty sore, sometimes for much longer than I used to when I was younger.

I'll never be the fastest or the strongest at my box, and that bothers me, but not the way it used to. I am getting stronger and faster, compared to where I was when I started. Sometimes I do need courage to face a workout (Murph was a particularly scary one ;) but not the kind of courage or fortitude it takes to tackle a

15 mile run all alone.

I've been told over and over again that CrossFit is dangerous, that I'll get injured. I just don't know what people are talking about when they say that to me. We spend a lot of time every workout going over correct form, and all the coaches pay attention to all of us, to be sure we don't get injured.

They watch each other performing workouts as well, so it seems crazy to me to criticise CrossFit as potentially dangerous. I've been sore after workouts definitely, sometimes where getting out of bed the next morning has become a bit of a trial, but I've never been injured. And when I've been sore, there's always someone at the box who will show me a really effective stretch or recommend a particular exercise to either ease soreness, or help strengthen a muscle so that I won't be sore that particular way again.

On days when someone in my class is very sore, the coaches recommend we take it easy that day: lighter weights, fewer repetitions, or an alternative movement altogether. It feels the exact opposite of dangerous. It feels safe.

The safety of CrossFit extends to the mental and emotional side of working out in a box (as a psychotherapist, this is always of interest to me). It's friendly in the box.

The fittest members and the least fit members are not

divided by their relative fitness nor anything else. Everyone is just there to get their work done, and we're equally encouraging of each other. I have never been inside a gym with an attitude from its members like this before! This in turn makes it okay not to be the fastest or the strongest.

On the *CrossFit Iron Duke* blog, we've had some amazing member posts — and I've read about how some members have struggled with their health, too. Which makes it safe for me to engage in all the things I have to do to manage my disease.

*****

Caroline Nairn is a CrossFit enthusiast, Psychotherapist and Advanced EFT Practitioner, specialising in using EFT to help with chronic disease and chronic pain, and improve sports performance. www.carolinenairn.com

Story Thirty-Nine

Brooke Bevan

I woke up early and sorted through a drawer of Lululemon, asking myself, *"Do I wear my new tights?... No, wear shorts, it's too hot."* Little did I know that that decision would save those new tights' life.

I was training at an exclusive functional fitness gym. It was hard, almost impossible at times, but I loved it. We were always challenged and on this morning we were working as a team on short intervals, high reps of box jumps, rowing and pull ups.

It was the kind of gym that you didn't ask questions. If you couldn't do something, don't ask, just do it. Or try. Never cry in public.

We completed the box jumps and rowing as fast as we could but we still had a team beating us.

It came to my turn on pull-ups. The bars were so high we needed a box to be able to reach them. I went to kip and on the way back, my hand slipped.

All that went through my head, in the split second of free falling was, *"Oh no.. this is going to hurt."*

Then came the impact. I don't remember a lot. I know that I let out a loud whimper as my body made contact with the ground. I knocked myself out. And as I came to, everyone was crowded around me. The pain blurred my vision. I was confused and disoriented and all I wanted to do was get up and run away.

That's the funny thing about pain. It's suffocating. You can't escape it. No matter how much morphine you are given, it still lingers. The only difference is that with morphine it takes longer for your brain to register the pain. It dulls the thought of the pain, but not the pain itself. No, that stays.

I was rushed to hospital, and it's funny the things that you remember.

Firstly, the horror and lack of acceptance when I was

told they were going to cut my lulu's off — thank god I didn't wear my new tights. Secondly, the intern ER doctor who decided to practice putting a cannula in my wrist and failing miserably multiple times — I had a deep, loathing hatred for her at that moment. Then there was the frustration that no one would give me a drink of water. I was so damn thirsty and the best they could do was put ice on my lips. And the complete denial, after the results of the x-rays and CT scans.

I honestly thought they had mixed my scans up...

I had an unstable burst and chance fracture to my T12. In layman's terms, my vertebra basically shattered into multiple pieces. I had an almost complete fracture to my occipital bone, a brain hemorrhage, I had managed to tear almost my entire left toenail off, and I had dislocated my right shoulder.

I was transferred to the trauma unit and I came in and out of my concussion as the specialists rolled through. I was told my skull would heal without intervention, but the hemorrhage would mean I wouldn't be able to smell anything for about six months. The spinal fracture needed to be stabilised, which meant surgery on my spine. Not something, even in my concussed state, that I would accept.

After discussions with my surgeon I had two choices: Surgery, or lie in bed for three months without any guarantee my fracture would heal. One thing that could be guaranteed was complete paralysis from my belly button down if it didn't heal.

I have never been so terrified of anything in my life. Through a face full of tears my only request before going into surgery was, *"Please make sure I can walk at the end of this."*

The surgery was a success, and within a few days I was fitted to a jewett brace and the physiotherapists came around to teach me how to get out of bed. The next day I had to try to walk. And the next, the physio asked me to attempt a lap around the ward, following me closely with a wheel chair. I did two.

Upon being discharged, the weeks and months that followed were tough but every day something improved, whether it meant I could stand up for a few minutes longer, or I could make it the whole way around the block without crying or having to get my partner to run home to get the car to pick me up.

It wasn't easy. It actually sucked. A lot.

I wanted to be back to normal immediately. I wanted to be back into training and make a remarkable comeback to my normal level of activity in the shortest amount of time possible. I had a Rocky montage rolling in my head most days.

Unfortunately, I set some unrealistic goals for my progress and when things didn't happen as I had decided they should, it felt like I had been smacked in the face. I had to accept I would never be what I perceived as "normal."

I had a severe injury that I will have to manage for the remainder of my life. My spine would never heal to its pre-injury state. I have a semi-permanent titanium implant in my spine that kept me walking, a vertebra that still looks like a crushed piece of honeycomb, and a guaranteed prognosis of further surgery in the future.

What it came down to was attitude. Being grateful for the baby steps that I was able to make. Setting realistic goals that were a little less rigid, a little more fluid. And not being in such a rush to recover and get back to the things that I have the rest of my life to do. Much easier said than done.

The hardest part for me wasn't the pain or the recovery but the mental struggle. I was diagnosed with Post-Traumatic Stress Disorder. Now on top of dealing with the injury, I also had panic attacks, flashbacks of the accident and the experiences in hospital, irrational meltdowns if I was under time pressure, and to top it off, I would burst into tears over what appeared to be, to the objective outsider, the most insignificant circumstances.

I was constantly battling adrenalin and that primal, uncontrollable instinct to pop-smoke and leg-it out of a situation immediately. Yes, I have literally run away from situations before, which can seem a little dramatic to the observer. The trigger can be anything. The hardest thing to explain to people is that I can't control it. Most of the time I have no idea what is happening, I just know that I need to escape.

I was accepted into a Bachelor of Physiotherapy program three days after acquiring the injury. This was one of the toughest tests of all, and still is.

Being in a learning environment that is about how to assist people in similar positions to what I was in, to learn in depth about the severity of spinal cord injuries and being in a hospital environment is a continual challenge.

Even though the flashbacks lessen with intensity the more I confront my feelings, unfortunately, they are still there.

It has also been an intense kind of therapy trying to disconnect as the patient and become the therapist.

I am not one to give up easily and I am known for my very stubborn, bull-headed attitude. If someone tells me I can't, I will go out of my way to prove that I can.

Since my accident just over a year ago, I have opened my own CrossFit gym. I think owning the gym, being in control of that environment, and setting my own pace for my workouts has been the only reason I have stepped back into CrossFit.

The best thing for my injury is to stay strong so that when I do need surgery, my recovery can be as fast and amazing as my last. Also, by having the muscle to support my skeletal system, I remain relatively pain-free most days.

After recently seeing my surgeon, expecting some stern words that I needed to reduce my training, I got the exact opposite. My spine is looking healthier than it did last year, which was before I started CrossFit training again.

CrossFit is an amazing training method and without it I don't feel that my progress and my recovery from such a severe injury would have been anywhere near as extraordinary as it has been. Even more important is the CrossFit community, both inside the box and in the greater community. I am very blessed to have been able to help forge an amazing community with a bunch of likeminded people. It is seeing them push themselves to their limits every day that inspires me. We all share a laugh and sometimes there are tears, but knowing that everyone is going through the same struggle is what gets us through.

I look back now and I see how far I have come and all the people who helped me get to where I am today. It is remarkable how the body can heal and adapt. How the human spirit can carry on, despite adversity.

With a little bit of stubbornness, an attitude to never give up, and some hard work, you can honestly achieve anything. I think I am the luckiest girl on earth.

*****

Brooke is a Musculoskeletal therapist and Physiotherapy student, and Owner and Coach of CrossFit 4000 in Brisbane, Australia. She is passionate about promoting a healthy way of living and enhancing the quality of life for others through functional movement, mobility and positive lifestyle habits.

Story Forty

Christina L. Atti-Uptegrow

I've been an athlete my whole life. Softball, basketball, soccer, and finding, in my later years, rugby and CrossFit.

This role came with some sort of pain associated with each day. I remember days of agony following a Saturday rugby game, only to hope that by Tuesday I would be back on the pitch for practice. In 2011, our team went on to win a National title, which was amazing to be part of.

I was an athlete; however, a couple of months afterwards I was at work and after walking up three flights of stairs I found myself winded. I had let myself go and needed to find myself again.

I had heard of CrossFit, but I questioned if it was for me. So I tried it, knowing I needed something more than the ordinary gym. I picked the box closest to the house and went to Foundations. *I. Was. Hooked.*

What I thought would be a couple of months became years. What was my sport has now become my career. It is the community; it is the seeing how the work pays off, and experiencing success, just like I had on the rugby field.

CrossFit brings out one's weaknesses, and eventually, through the work put in, makes those weaknesses successes.

I was getting stronger every day, and my body was becoming what I had never even known I would want. I was the girl with a six-pack. I would WOD five to six days a week. I was sleeping better, my nutrition was on track with the rest of my life choices, and I was feeling great.

Then it happened. The pain I associated with everyday life was no longer manageable. It started sometime in September 2014, where my rest days started to outnumber my training days. On October 8, 2014, I reluctantly drove to work having not slept much of the night before and I could not sit, walk, stand, or sway myself into a comfortable position.

I went to urgent care. The doctor there suggested Physical Therapy. He clearly told me that the shooting pain down my leg and up through my neck needed attention, that lower back pain is not something I should just deal with. My physical therapist met with me and took most exercise movements away.

My new exercise program was a series of stretches and rest, to attempt to calm down the nerve pain I was experiencing. I would go to the box and do my stretches as my fellow athletes would WOD. I was constantly being asked if I was okay, because it wasn't like me to not push myself in the box.

I expected a lot from my body. I felt like I was getting better, the pain was subsiding, but I now know the amount of medicine I was taking masked what I was truly feeling. It was not going away; I was building a tolerance.

In January 2015, I was back to adding more movements to my training. I would attempt to add one movement, and if I didn't feel pain the next day, I was okay to keep it on my regimen. Not many made it to the approved list.

Through the pain, I competed in a competition I had signed up for months prior, with support from my PT. Not my best idea, but it was fun, and I got to compete with my wife, who won the strength WOD for our team. It was her first competition, and I was so proud of her.

In January, I switched boxes, being hired as a Community Outreach Coordinator and Coach at a different CrossFit affiliate. CrossFit was now my passion in my personal and professional life. Being a CrossFit coach was always something I strived for, given that I have loved coaching softball and rugby in the past.

I was no longer just a CrossFit athlete, but a coach, athlete and mentor for this group of athletes.

I was beyond excited about my new path, and I truly believe everything happens for a reason. Even though my life was going in the right direction, on February 13th, 2015, I looked at my wife and said, *"I can't do this anymore."*

The pain was now shooting into my lower legs on both sides; I couldn't sit down, walking was a huge struggle, and my back was in agony. The movements I could handle were minimal.

The initial doctor said it was bursitis, gave me a shot, and sent me on my way. I was scheduled to see him six weeks later. I made it five days and was back for another appointment. The long process of doctors, x-rays, MRIs, stronger and stronger medications, and rest unfolded.

On March 20, 2015, I would finally meet with a surgeon who discussed my prognosis and options. My options were few. At this point I was using my left leg like a peg, my right was not far behind in the pain scale. Nerve pain would keep me awake, I took 15-plus pills a day to function and I could not complete other normal functions of everyday life.

It was clear that surgery was my only choice. Continuing to lose function in my leg could result in permanent nerve damage or complete loss of function in my leg. This was not an option.

I was at the box everyday despite being at such a low point. At home I would say, *"I can't do this any more"* in tears, and my wife would tell me how inspirational I was, and how I truly had no other choice but to keep moving forward.

This would empower me to be the best I could be for the athletes I was coaching. I would be at the box, and every class brought about inquiries about my prognosis, and how they could help me through this trying time.

While awaiting surgery, I had to coach more through verbal cues than my body, using athletes in my classes to demonstrate good movement. They were great, and more than understanding. It was like each athlete was taking part of my pain, and they were making it their own. I was not alone.

Each person would then tell me their story of conquest, and how they too are healing old wounds. CrossFit will show you strengths, and bring out your weaknesses, when pushed to move correctly. We learn where we have been compensating for so long.

April 7th, 2015 finally came, and I have been humbled at having to learn how to do things all over again. My pain was relieved immediately. I now know I was dealing with a herniated disc for 10-plus years.

I am now forced to allow myself to heal, and I will be stronger in the years to come; at least, that is how I see it. I am humbled at the minimal functions I can accomplish; however, I am empowered by the messages, outreach, and love I have received from my CrossFit community.

Every day the athletes are part of my recovery and part of my motivation. Our bodies are amazing, and while humbled right now, I am so thankful to know a time without pain.

*****

Christina Atti-Uptegrow is a coach and Community Outreach coordinator for Raleigh CrossFit.

Story Forty-One

Aaron D. Taylor

I had always been into fitness growing up. Surfing, skim boarding, soccer, life guarding — you name it, I probably tried it at least once.

It was just like any other day. I was 19 at the time and was doing "iron work" on a construction site. I remember that morning pretty well. I woke up, showered, got dressed and had some fruit with my father like any other day, then argued with my older brother about who was taking the leftover spaghetti for lunch — ha!

I got in my truck around 5:45am, heading to work, and then all I remember was waking up in Halifax Hospital in Daytona Beach, Florida. I had been put in a sedated coma for nine days.

I woke up to find out that I was in a head-on car accident caused by a distracted driver. My truck was split into two and was rolled multiple times.

I had a long list of injuries: I broke my right ankle in three places, snapped my right femur in half and lost two out of my six pints of blood, and my left collarbone was broken.

I fractured my neck and dislocated my jaw, which was

wired shut for two months; broke my nose; and shattered both eye sockets. They had to remove my face to reconstruct it. I needed 100 staples in my head. The right eye socket was replaced with titanium/medical metal and the left side was reconstructed with steel mesh because they were able to salvage some of the bone fragments from my face.

Along with all this head trauma, I was told I may have Short Term Memory Loss (STML). My eyes were blood red from my face crashing against the steering wheel.

I ended up getting laser surgery on my eyes. I had to be awake for this procedure and it was one of the most painful 15 minutes of my life. My eyes were so damaged that the glasses I was prescribed had lenses that were about a quarter inch thick. The doctor said he'd give me a few more months to see if my eyes would continue to recover before another surgery.

When I returned for that check-up, even though I was lip reading, the Doctor very clearly dropped the F-bomb. He said, *"You don't need surgery any more. You healed better than I ever imagined you would."* It was truly a blessing. I had friends and family all over the world praying for me.

I remember waking up to my doctor asking if I believed in God. I replied with a *"yes sir, I do."* He said I sure hope so because someone was looking out for you. Weeks had gone by and he told me there was a chance I would never compete in any sport again and a chance that I'd never walk "normal."

I remember that when my doctors told me all of this stuff, I had smiled and laughed. I replied, "*My God is good and he'll heal me to the way he wants me to be.*" It wasn't easy. I knew things happened for a reason; that's just how God works.

At this point, a year and a half had gone by. I saw the CrossFit Games on TV and said, *"I want to do that."* That was how I was going to reach my goals and get back to being "normal."

I found the closest box to my house and started as soon as I was able to. I proved my doctors wrong!

That five foot, eight inches, 125 pound young man that struggled with walking is now 175 pounds and can run a mile in under six minutes and 30 seconds, and can clean and jerk 340, snatch 275, deadlift 500 pounds for 10 reps, and back squat 450 pounds.

I knew through God and CrossFit, I could reach my goals! My drive for the Lord and fitness has never been so powerful in my life as since my car accident.

While I was in the hospital, my mother and a friend gave me a Bible verse that I've never let go of and that keeps me on track:

"You intended to harm me, but God intended it all for good. He brought me to this position so I could save the

lives of many people." (Genesis 50:20 NLT)

"For I know the plans I have for you," says the LORD. "They are plans for good and not for disaster, to give you a future and a hope." (Jeremiah 29:11 NLT)

"Jesus looked at them intently and said, 'Humanly speaking, it is impossible. But with God everything is possible." (Matthew 19:26 NLT)

From facing this horrible time in my life, I learned one thing: Be sure to put God first before anything else because He is good and will never leave you alone.

Story Forty-Two

Courtney Kroen

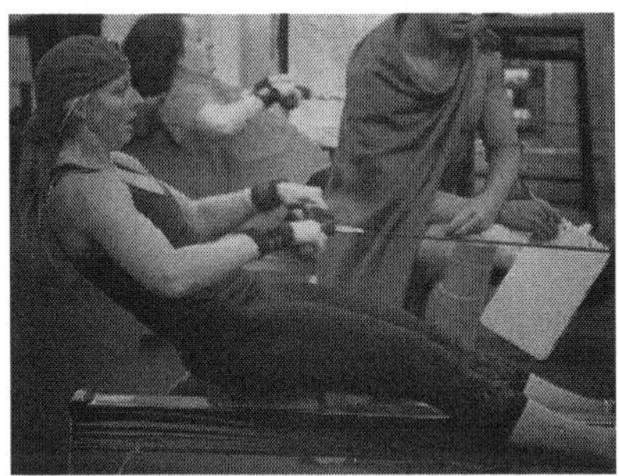

"A moment in time" — four words spoken to me from one of my CrossFit coaches during a dark time in my life. These words stuck and have not left my side since. These four words got me through to where I am today and helped me to overcome a number of setbacks along the way.

Two years ago I found this thing I love. Something that takes both everything from me — physically, emotionally, and mentally — then gives me back even more than I had before.

This past year I found myself injured and the weakest I have ever been.

Today, I am stronger than ever and have my *CrossFit*

Crux family to thank. They never stopped motivating, encouraging, supporting, and inspiring me.

A dark 6am morning in October, 2013, a collective group of us heard the familiar, *"3-2-1 ... GO!"* and within moments there was a crash onto the floor from the rig. Hours later, I found out I had shattered my elbow into multiple pieces and the subsequent force of the impact also broke my wrist.

I was heading into surgery without an understanding of just how much this would change my life in the future. Many things that I loved were taken from me. CrossFit. Teaching. Painting. I was left with inexplicable pain and a life lived in four hour increments until I could have another round of pain killers.

The year following was a series of mini successes...

A close friend would provide me with weekly goals, such as opening a yogurt, being able to put my hair up in a ponytail, and making my infamous "peace" sign. Each of these were menial tasks for most, but were major challenges that I worked at and cried over daily.

How I missed the sound of barbells hitting the floor. The sweet day came in February 2014, when I was well enough to make my way over to *CrossFit Crux* just to listen to that sound I missed and to sit on the Airdyne as I used my rehab putty to waken up the nerves in my hand again.

This was my new WOD and varying putty consistencies were my new PRs.

As the months progressed, I learned, with the help of my coaches, how to modify EVERYTHING. Their knowledge, support, and patience speaks volumes to the CrossFit community and dedication of its coaches. I felt like a burden every day and hated asking for every aspect of the WOD to be modified and scaled.

They never wavered and were always happy to help and ensure I was included. Tasks that were once second nature to me — holding the lightest kettlebell, racking the training bar, or supporting my own body weight in a plank — were now humbling and devastating experiences.

I will never forget front squatting one day early on in my recovery and being completely discouraged by the 55 pounds I had on the bar. Knowing my legs and body were more than strong enough, but how incredibly difficult it was for me to even support the weight with my arm elevated to a rack position. My coach came over to encourage me to suck it up and just squat, only to find me with tears streaming down my face. This was not a one off.

This re-telling seems like a nightmare from another lifetime, but is perhaps a blessing in disguise, which forced me to slow my life down, find the belief in myself that had been missing, and learn that it was okay to lean on the support from those who constantly picked me up, ensured me of my progress when I wasn't seeing it, and fostered my sense of perseverance.

I made it a point to throw my heart into my rehab and into every workout regardless of how mentally taxing or discouraging it was — knowing what I had been capable of once upon a time.

How far we have all come, regardless of each individual journey. This is a gentle reminder to anyone struggling with a challenge in their life to remember that it is only "a moment in time."

*****

Courtney is a high school teacher and coach. She continues to train in CrossFit and sets new PRs and goals every day!

Story Forty-Three

Christine Stevens

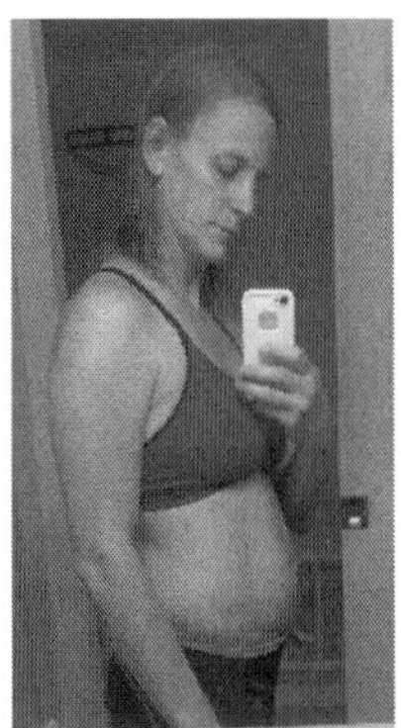

I have always been an athlete (field hockey, volleyball, softball, Muay Thai, boxing, and rugby) and I always love a good challenge. I began CrossFit in 2009 when I was training for my first Muay Thai competition and needed to cut weight. I was told that CrossFit would help me in the ring.

I remember my first workout; it had running, thrusters, and kettlebell swings in it. I hated every minute of it in one sense, and in the next I absolutely loved it! It taxed every part of my body and my mind. This is the day that my passion for CrossFit began.

In 2011, I wanted to do more and decided to get my

Level 1. That was the most exhilarating experience. I have been coaching ever since, beginning at *CrossFit Summerville,* then *Muskegon CrossFit,* and now at *Delaware CrossFit.*

The CrossFit community really drew me in. I became pregnant and the community really surrounded me with their love. I was still coaching and training during my pregnancy. I ended up gaining more weight throughout my pregnancy than I expected.

The day my daughter was born, I taught two ladies a foundations class and I was doing 95 pound power cleans. I remember the ladies asked me when I was due and I told them that I was only eight months. Less than one week before this, I was told that I had elevated blood pressure levels.

The day that my daughter was born, my blood pressure had spiked 180/110.

My daughter was four weeks early and was in NICU for 15 days. The CrossFit community provided meals for my family while my daughter was in the hospital. It was a blessing.

After delivering my daughter, I was required to take blood pressure medication. I have never had issues with my blood pressure; if anything, it was always low (115/70). I was 205 pounds the day I had my daughter and I dropped to 180 pounds (2012).

I was so disappointed that I had gained that much weight that I was determined to make a change and get back to my pre-pregnancy weight and get off of blood pressure medication.

I hit the CrossFit box five to six days per week and changed my diet. Within six months, I was able to eliminate blood pressure medication permanently and I haven't needed it since. Within two years, I was able to drop down to 145 pounds.

CrossFit has defined my weaknesses and also my strengths. It has enabled me to become a better person physically and mentally. It has helped me to challenge myself and inspire and encourage others to reach their goals. The community assisted me during recovery from foot surgery, even when I wasn't able to WOD with them.

CrossFit is the most amazing community, far more positive and supportive than any other sport that I have been involved in. I want to inspire my daughter to dream big and reach for the stars, that all goals are possible and attainable.

CrossFit has also led me to a deeper passion for nutrition and fitness. I want to help others to achieve their goals, and to get off of medications through the foods they eat and the workouts they do.

I went to Integrative Nutrition and obtained my Health Coaching Certification and began INSPIRE

Health and Fitness to help my clients reach their goals and find success in all areas of life.

*****

Christine Stevens is a coach at Delaware Crossfit and owner of INSPIRE Health and Fitness: www.inspirehealthandfitness.us

Story Forty-Four

Michelle Beauchamp

In January of 2010, I was given the news that I was a BRCA1 carrier. This means that I am a breast cancer gene carrier and if I did not seek radical preventative measures, I would have a 90% chance of developing breast and ovarian cancer.

Those words hit me like a tonne of bricks...

My mother had died of ovarian cancer when I was a teen and I had just watched my two sisters go through chemotherapy and radiation a year prior for breast and ovarian cancer. I left the doctor's office feeling confused and anxious about what to do next.

I had always been active. I had a gym membership and tried to stay healthy, knowing that cancer was in my family. I had heard about CrossFit and attended my first introductory class, falling in love immediately. Shortly thereafter was when I tested positive for the BRCA1 gene.

I researched online to educate myself about my options and worked closely with the hospital counsellor who shared her knowledge and guidance. I went on to blogs to learn how other women my age (35) were dealing with this diagnosis and with the help and support of my husband, I decided to have the double mastectomy and reconstructive surgery done as soon as possible.

I would have surgery to remove my ovaries later on. I knew I wanted to stay alive for as long as I could and be a mom to my son. I had lost my mother at such a young age and I didn't want that same thing to happen to my child. I had to get ahead of the cancer before it got to me.

Having the knowledge that I was a carrier was a blessing. This enabled me to take preventative

measures that my mother was not afforded.

Knowledge is power. I did not want to be worried every day, waiting for it to happen — every mammogram, every pain in my breast, wondering if it was cancer.

My first major surgery was in November of 2010. This process needed follow up appointments with my plastic surgeon every three weeks for a small procedure. This went on for about six months.

My second surgery occurred in June of 2011. Everything went well, and I felt relieved that I didn't have to worry so much any more. My chances of getting breast cancer had decreased by 90%. The procedure does not completely remove all of your tissue so there is a small chance of developing cancer despite the surgery.

Although I was relieved, part of me felt self-conscious about how my breasts looked. In order to remove the most tissue possible, the incision was made running straight across each breast. When I am fully clothed, the physical scars do not show.

However, at this point in my life, my self-esteem was at an all time low and my emotional scars were there day in and day out.

Just looking in the mirror reminded me of how my body had been permanently changed. It just wasn't fair. Cancer had taken my amazing mother from me, had put my sisters through hell, and now it had left me with scars running across my chest and breasts that would never be the same. I just didn't feel the confidence that I once felt before the surgery.

I listened to my friends talk about how much they loved CrossFit and how their bodies were responding; they were becoming stronger, not only beautiful but powerful as well. They sounded so empowered and confident. They had also met many new friends along the way. I knew it was time. I had my biggest surgery out of the way and I was healed and ready to try something different, and I am so glad I did.

I joined my local CrossFit box in the fall of 2011. It was not long after that, that I began feeling stronger every day. The workouts and Olympic Lifting were giving me more confidence than I ever could have imagined.

I knew I had another surgery coming up to remove my ovaries and that would put me into complete menopause at age 36, and this had me very concerned. I knew I had to do it to keep ahead of cancer, but I was afraid of what my life would be like once my body was forced into this major life change, well before it's time.

The gynecologists I saw told me, *"Everyone is different, we can't tell you how you will feel, how you will react. The side effects of menopause can be very bad, troubled sleep patterns, hot flashes, mood swings, low sex drive..."*

All this scared me to death, even more than having the double mastectomy had. I continued to train through CrossFit five times a week. I knew I needed the support I had found in the gym community to help me through the process.

For one hour a day, I was able to leave all my worries behind. It was just me competing against myself, working to be stronger than I was the day before, and fighting to get to the finish and find new limits.

In June of 2013 I had surgery to remove my ovaries and tubes. The procedure was a success and I recovered well. I believe that going into the surgery with a strong mind and body helped me recover much faster than the average person.

I couldn't wait to get back to the gym, where I felt empowered and encouraged by my CrossFit family.

I was worried about how my strength would change without my hormones but honestly, if anything, I have gotten stronger since my surgery. So many things that I was worried about and warned about do not affect me. I am in menopause and some things are different.

I do get many hot flashes and mood swings but these are side effects I can live with. To me they are minor inconveniences. I truly believe it's because of my strong CrossFit body that I have been able to recover and adapt so well. CrossFit is my emotional outlet and it has helped with my mindset. It's helped me feel strong and not worry about my scars or how I look in the mirror. CrossFit and its community have given me hope.

CrossFit changed my life in so many ways. My journey in the last four years has been incredible. I continue to learn Olympic Lifting and I am working out beyond what I thought I was capable of. The coaches and the other members encourage everyone through each workout. The atmosphere is so positive and the friends I have made along the way are incredible.

Guess what? Over these four years of CrossFit, I have stopped worrying about how I look in the mirror. My scars don't even bother me because I feel strong and healthy. Mentally, CrossFit has given me my confidence back, it has challenged me to get stronger, lift heavier, and run faster. It makes me feel powerful, and for me, that is priceless.

Story Forty-Five

Tara Kinney

As I stood there staring at my reflection in the mirror, my first response was the all too familiar wave of disgust...My eyes scanned over the 250 pounds that were draped uncomfortably over my 5 ft 5 in frame, and I looked at myself with disdain and embarrassment.

Standing there next to the pile of clothes on the floor that I could no longer squeeze into, I began to cut off the top of my overalls so that I had something to wear.

Then something happened and I remember it as if

it were yesterday...

I again looked up at the mirror, but this time I gazed directly into my eyes. For the first time in a long time, I looked past the surface, past the hurt, past the defeat, and I saw strength. As my mind cleared, a new wave of determination came over me and I made a vow right then that I was going to take back control.

The road to change was not easy or fast, but as I started committing to small incremental improvements, celebrating wins, consistently moving the bar and setting new goals, I began paving the way toward transformation.

The first roadblock I had to break through was my own internal narrative. I had collected 18 years of negativity, recorded it, and replayed it back to myself repeatedly.

My step-dad making noises while I ate or booming sounds when I walked, my grandmother pointing out how large I looked on stage at my recital, a boy in seventh grade pretending he liked me so he could lure me to a table where kids wrote TGIF (Tara Gagliardo is Fat) all over pieces of paper and laughed at me, the soccer coach telling me I didn't have what it took, the dozens of times I had heard I had "a pretty face." The list went on and on.

As I began reflecting on my personal journey, my mother's words from a recent Facebook post kept coming back to me.

"The words 'quit and can't' are not in this woman's vocabulary. She possesses some amazing skills and talents — but nothing can compare to her awesome heart!"

If it were not for my determination, my dedication to the journey — my heart — I would have quit long ago. I continuously battled my negative self-talk head on and was slowly able to prove those words wrong.

I changed my nutritional habits one at a time, slowly added more and more physical activity, and I made steady progress. The day I started college, I was down 50 pounds and my confidence was on the rise.

Taking off the next 30 pounds was a slower process, but by the end of college I was holding steady at 170. It wasn't my goal, but I was 80 pounds lighter than when I had started!

After college, my weight fluctuated up and down a bit, but I held fairly steady on the same plateau. I met an amazing man that I am blessed to call my husband and we had our first little girl, Ashley, in 2010.

Throughout my pregnancy, those negative voices I had worked hard to quiet, began speaking up. I worked hard to maintain healthy eating and exercise, but I was still scared of being "fat" again.

Embracing the determination that had come to define

me, I made a post-baby goal to run a half marathon and, when Ashley was five months old, I did just that. Although I was pumped that I had conquered this goal, I still could not manage to get those last 20 pounds off to reach my "healthy weight."

As I chatted with a friend at church about my frustration and how I didn't think I could conquer this last part of the journey alone, a woman sitting in front of us turned around and told me, *"I've got something perfect for you!"*

This was a chance meeting that would make a huge change in my life!

Up to this point, I had achieved personal goals through self-motivation and affirmation from my friends and family. This had taken me a long way, but I was stagnant and needed more. What I did not have was the support of people traveling a similar wellness journey with me. I found this in CrossFit.

I was blessed to have met Nicole that day at church and to be welcomed with open arms into the *CrossFit SolaFide* family. I have continued to be blessed by the amazing CrossFit community each time the Army has taken us on a new adventure.

As cliché as it may sound, the camaraderie and inclusive support found within CrossFit is not bound within the walls of any one "box." I have rooted myself in a few CrossFit homes over the past few years, and the culture is not isolated. No matter where I have dropped in, I find a community embedded with the commitment to help people find where they are today, set short and long term goals, and cheer on every achievement made or milestone reached.

Being a part of this amazing culture that reinforces holistic wellness and brings continuously varied challenges, combined with my drive to build a stronger temple for the Lord, helped me to finally reach 100 POUNDS LOST!

That was three years ago and I continue to make new gains and improvements every day!

Working out on your own, you can easily stay in one place. The cohesive fellowship that I found in CrossFit not only motivated me to improve myself, but drove the collective group to improve together.

On my own I likely would have either remained on that plateau, or worse, I could have lost my motivation and declined. The CrossFit community consistently challenged me to test the perimeters of my comfort zone, push against the edges of my abilities, defy the status quo, remain open to new challenges, and continuously make incremental improvements.

Being a part of this culture, I know that I will never plateau again because any time I get comfortable, I will be pushed to new limits. This continual growth will be a driving force in my life to sustain change. I believe in this so strongly, that I am now a CrossFit Level 1 Trainer dedicated to helping others on their wellness journeys.

Whatever you do, work at it with all your heart, as though you were working for the Lord and not people.
~ Colossians 3:23

*****

Tara is a proud military wife and mother of two young girls. She is an entrepreneur committed to Leadership Development, Physical Fitness, and Holistic Wellness. Tara feels blessed to now have the opportunity to help others through their journeys.

Her strong faith in God has not only strengthened her own approach to staying healthy, but has strengthened Tara's purpose of relating to and helping others through similar struggles.

Story Forty-Six

B.W.

I remember the first day I walked into what I now call the Box. The smell of people sweating filled my nose, and all I could hear were people grunting, breathing hard, and a few random "woots" and people yelling, *"Keep going! You're almost there!"*

Unlike the traditional gym setting I was used to, this place was more rugged and had an industrial feel to it. The building had numerous large garage bay doors and there were high ceilings throughout.

I was nervous and intimidated, but this is where my story begins.

I had always been someone who worked out but in a more traditional gym setting, so when I first heard about CrossFit, I was a little uneasy about trying it. I was more of a solo gym goer. I did not like the thought of going to a "class," also referred to as a "WOD."

After talking about it to my best friend, she convinced me to go check it out. I walked in those doors, pushed through my nerves, and did the first workout. I have been hooked ever since!

I officially joined CrossFit and realized it wasn't a "class" — it was a group of people striving for the same thing. Everyone was there reaching for their own personal best in performance, and when you were doing the workouts, the only person you were paying attention to was yourself.

At every WOD I was focused on getting through it and pumping myself up to do so. I would motivate myself by telling myself, "*You got this! Just a few more reps! You're almost there! You can breathe later!*" It was a mind over matter game and if I just listened to myself, I always succeeded.

I met some amazing people; specifically, a really good girlfriend who welcomed me into her CrossFit community. We would get together outside of the box, hang out, grab a bite, and chat. For me this was one of the best parts.

I was not originally from the area and did not know a ton of people so being surrounded by these positive, motivating people was not only amazing but they were a wakeup call for me.

At that time in my life, I was not happy. I could find a piece of happiness while at the Box or when I was with other CrossFitters, but at home, I was in a miserable relationship and I hated the job I was in.

I kept doing CrossFit and the more I did it and the more I saw these new friends, the more I realized that I had to make my own happiness. So I decided to start focusing on finding a new job. I started the process of applying to the Police Service.

CrossFit helped me to grow my confidence as well as my strength and endurance and I decided that if I was going to do this, I was going to do it now! The weeks and months went by and I went through the Police hiring process, the physical, practical, and written tests. Then after what seemed like forever, I was hired and went away for a grueling three months of training.

CrossFit kept me focused; every weekend I was home I would re-center myself and find myself again at the Box getting my CrossFit fix in.

I successfully completed training and was about to start my new job as a Police Officer. The job was amazing! I loved every minute of it! Although I was now happy with my job, the relationship I was in was still there, like a dark cloud hanging over me.

I had changed my career and reached my goals but that had been the easier of the two. While focusing on my new job and all the training that went with it, I would forget about the relationship and how bad it was. I thought maybe things would get better with a better job, but that was not the case. The relationship was only getting worse. I had got to the point where I was happier to be at work than I was to be at home.

I wanted to do anything but be at home in the negative environment with my boyfriend. It was like I had become two different people. I would act like I was happy and everything was okay at work, and sometimes even try and convince myself that everything was okay. When it came to going home though, reality would set in and I was overwhelmed and felt trapped, suffocating emotionally.

I tried to fight through the pain and the hurt he made me feel, but it was a constant battle trying to convince myself that everything was fine. I would cry myself to sleep at night, get up the next day, hop in the car, and drive to work, putting on a smile and pretending everything was great.

A series of events took place that summer after joining the force and I finally hit the ceiling of what I could take. I decided I had to get out. I did not like the person I was becoming and, even worse, my friends and family were noticing. I couldn't hide it any more.

The end was a struggle and, just like I had learned in CrossFit, I had to coach and encourage myself to stick with my choice. I had to keep giving myself the pep talk saying, *"No, you can't do this any more, don't fall back into trying it again,"* because it never works and nothing ever changes.

As the weeks and months went on, things started to get a bit easier. The relationship was now over and I started moving forward with my life and moved back to the area I loved. I found a perfect little place in the country to start over. I was starting to feel like myself again and I was smiling because I wanted to, not to cover anything up.

I was fortunate to have my family and, of course, some friends from CrossFit come help me move.

This is the part, looking back, that always gives me chills...

My good girlfriend, whom I first met at CrossFit, was one of the people that came to help. She brought her awesome hubby as well as her younger brother with her that day. Not only did CrossFit help me push through the personal struggles I have shared, CrossFit led me to the best guy I have ever known.

Yes, my girlfriend's brother. Shortly after the move, we started chatting and hanging out and just like that an amazing relationship was born. The best part is he also does CrossFit. So, now together we encourage, push and support each other in and outside of the box.

Things come into our lives for a reason and I know CrossFit came into my life to save me. Life is such an extraordinary adventure and I have learned when you do things that are best for YOU or you remove the toxic elements in your life, amazing things are then able to come to you without any struggle.

I am so thankful and couldn't be any happier. My life is now easy and I feel fulfilled. I don't think any of it would have happened without the determination and confidence that CrossFit gave me, not only in the gym but in every aspect of my life.

I will always remember visiting with my mom a few months after all these changes and she said that after eight years, she finally had her daughter back.

Story Forty-Seven

Anthea Childs

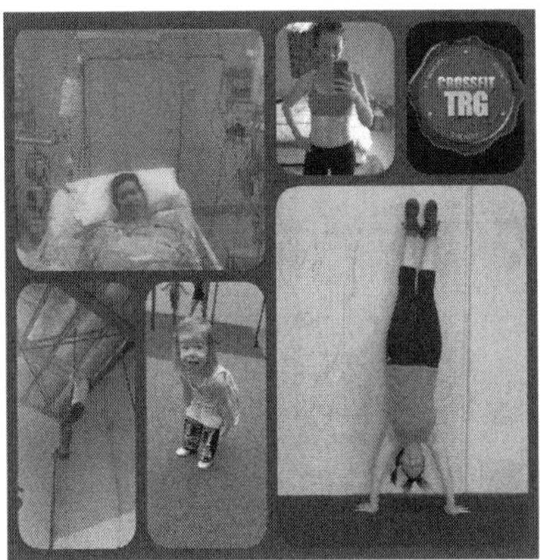

I remember looking at the class schedule at my local 24/7 gym in December 2013. There were the usual classes, but the one that stood out to me was one labelled "CrossFit." I had no idea at the time what it was, but I thought I would give it a go.

I wet myself during the warm up and I also ended up crying throughout the entire hour. Two years later, I look back at that day and smile, as I started so weak but now I feel the strongest I have ever felt in my entire life.

In late January 2013, I had my first baby. I welcomed

to the world a beautiful little girl; however, her birth resulted in life threatening complications. I suffered a massive postpartum hemorrhage that resulted in me being placed into an induced coma and put on life support. I required hours of surgery and a massive blood transfusion along with other blood products to keep me alive.

I was lucky. I fought to survive. I had a family now and they needed me.

I recovered well, my daughter was ticking all of the boxes, and I was allowed light exercise for a period of time. I was never really into fitness prior to having my daughter. The only reason I did exercise prior was to help get pregnant in the first place! I continued walking and light post-natal Pilates; however, it didn't really make me feel any better.

Eleven months after my daughter's birth, I needed to find something that made me feel better. After going through such a traumatic birth, I suffered bouts of depression and anxiety that were later identified as PND and PTSD. In December 2013, I was given the all clear to return to exercise and this is where I found myself looking at this "CrossFit" class.

I cried through my first session because I had wet myself after the coach had told me to go run. I didn't understand the extent having a baby would impact on many basic things like bladder control. I ended up just sitting on a spin bike for the remainder of the class, crying while everyone else did the workout.

I went back the next week, because the coaches had reached out to me, giving me scaling options, and the other participants had encouraged me to come back. I felt this overwhelming support that I hadn't received from anyone else.

In April 2014, we moved to *CrossFit TRG,* a massive CrossFit box with an amazing set up. I hadn't ever seen anything like it. There were pull-up bars and gymnastics rings. I felt like a kid all over again. I had found my comfort zone and continued to just do one or two sessions a week. I didn't have any specific goals at this point in time; it was nice to just get out of the house and be around people that were positive and just wanted to look after themselves.

In October 2014, I decided that it was time to become a little more committed and form some goals. Initially I wanted to lose the weight I had gained from poor eating and not being as active after having my daughter. I participated in a 30 day challenge, changed my diet, and moved to three CrossFit sessions and one gymnastics session a week.

My goals also changed towards the end of the challenge. I wasn't as interested in losing weight or being skinny. I just had this burning desire to become strong. Every week I was progressing, and I felt more focused and my desire to take CrossFit more seriously grew.

With this change, I also found that my head began to feel clearer. I felt more capable to cope with the demands of being a mum, a wife, and a part-time employee. I felt like I could control some of the darker feelings that were holding me back and that I could push myself like I had never done before.

The support around me was just amazing; in December 2014, a new coaching team had formed at *CrossFit TRG*. The community feel that this provided was not like anything I had experienced before and it was overwhelming how many members would listen to my story. It was more overwhelming how many other members became my friends and became those that inspired me to work harder towards my goals.

CrossFit TRG introduced an Athlete of the Month board at the beginning of the year. It is in the main entrance as you walk in. I looked at it and decided I wanted to work hard and be on that board by the end of the year. Not just for what I could do in a workout but for how I supported others.

While I focused on myself, I also ensured that I was a support to others that were around me.

In March 2015, I participated in the CrossFit Open — Scaled division. I wasn't 100% ready but I gave it everything I had. I even managed my first ever no-band pull-up in the Open! I PR'd in many areas and found a determination I never thought I had. Most of all, I was surrounded by people that cared for me and wanted to see me succeed.

The best moment was when I really struggled in one of the workouts. I cried for the entire eight minutes. When the workout was over, I had my friends come and hug me for trying so hard. It was a beautiful moment that showed me how proud people were of what I have achieved. In the same month, I was also awarded Athlete of the Month at *CrossFit TRG*, a goal that I wanted to achieve by the end of 2015!

CrossFit TRG, the coaches, and the members became my new family. I still do cry from time to time, but there is always someone there to give me a hug or high-five. Thankfully, I have the bladder issue under control as well!

I have a great coaching team around me that has helped me absolutely smash goals that I never thought were possible. I don't even know how to describe how changed I feel about myself, not just on the outside but the inside as well.

I hope that I inspire new members that come to TRG, as I am very open about how I went from being in a coma to tears and wetting myself to now being able to RX some WODs. All of this in less than two years.

I am extremely fortunate to have a husband and a family that are supportive of my CrossFit journey.

They enable me the time to train and help me with my daughter. My beautiful little girl has now started to show signs of being interested in what I do; this is something I will most certainly encourage.

I was given a second chance at life, the opportunity with a new life. Finding CrossFit has just enhanced the opportunity to make it the most amazing life ever. I just have to work for it!

Story Forty-Eight

Jon E.

I have dealt with weight issues for most of my life. I grew up with a single mom who worked her rear off to provide for me. Eating healthy at home was rare due to a very hectic schedule and the fact that she had little energy to put into cooking after a long day at work.

As a kid, I was very active and played a lot of sports. I was even pretty good at a few of them. However, as I grew up, I gained more and more weight, which led to more and more teasing.

I was over 300 pounds by the time I was 18. I would hide the hurt and would usually numb it by eating more. This continued into my adult life. I would feel the shame of my weight and would try this diet or that diet.

I would lose a little and then gain it all back, plus more.

I had a lot of great friends growing up, that saw past the weight. They meant everything to me. As we all got older, and they started to get married and have families of their own, I grew more and more lonely. I dreamt of being married and having a family someday, but never thought that anyone would want me. This led to more eating and other addictions to try to cover the loneliness and emptiness that I felt in life.

I started to gamble and became very addicted to the "high" of winning. I became "friends" with card dealers and other gambling addicts. I took value from them. In the casinos, I was treated as royalty because I spent so much time and money there. I never paid for a meal.

Then I lost everything I owned, and turned to stealing from the business that I ran with my best friend. I did this for almost 2 years until I realized that I couldn't hide it anymore. I confessed and brought it all into the light.

I had stolen from my best friend and from other close friends that had entrusted me with their business. I should have gone to jail, but by the mercy of God and my friends, I didn't.

At this point, I had hit rock bottom emotionally and financially. I had nothing.

I remember breaking down, on the floor of my apartment kitchen, wishing that I had a gun to end it all. I have no doubt that if one was there, I would have done it.

The shame of everything that I had done sent me into

deeper depression. I continued to cope with it by eating and spending time alone playing video games. The only time that I would leave my apartment was to go to a gambling addiction therapy group or to try to earn some money by taking pictures of repossessed homes for banks.

This continued until I hit 533 pounds. I could barely walk around. I was always short of breath. I had developed lymphedema and my legs were so swollen with fluid that I had to add fabric to my jean legs, just so that they could fit.

There finally came a day that I had to make a decision whether to continue to slowly die, or take my life back.

I couldn't bear the thought of leaving the ones that I loved, so I decided to get off my ass and change. The first area of change was getting a real job and beginning to pay back the money that I had stolen. I was fortunate and was able to find a great job that paid well.

As I began to take responsibility, I regained the friendships that I had lost, even from the same person that I stole directly from. Just writing that overwhelms me with the Grace of God.

A year and 4 months after I had hit rock bottom, that same friend that I had hurt so badly, recommended me for employment with someone that I had known for over 18 years. That man gave me a chance to really get back into a job that I loved. I was able to turn my life around financially and started to feel good about who I was again.

Once this happened, it led to wanting to become a healthier person. The inside was feeling better, so it was time to let that start showing on the outside. I had seen a couple of old gambling friends post comments on social media about how their lives had changed for the better and how they had started focusing on their health. I met with them and started working with them on my nutrition.

I started taking supplements and started paying attention to what I was eating. After doing this for a few months, I dropped about 50 pounds. I then began to take steps, literally, towards becoming active and exercising. I started walking and even signed up for an 8 mile "fun run" in my city.

It was the hardest thing that I had done physically, but I crossed that finish line and got my shirt (even though the shirt still wasn't big enough to fit).

After the race was complete, my boss saw that I was trying to figure out what to do for exercise next. He opened the door to a whole new world and showed me what would later become one of my strongest passions: CrossFit. He invited me to try a class with him. If I liked it, he would pay for me to continue through that summer, as a "benefit" for working for him.

I did the standard first timer workout; 3 rounds of 10 push ups, 10 sit ups and 10 air squats. It sucked and the next day, I was more sore than I was after an 8 mile walk. I wanted more.

I told my boss that I was "in" and began hitting a few classes per week. My strength was non-existent at first. I was struggling with lifts at 65 lbs. My mile time was over 24 minutes. I still loved it. Every time that I walked in, fellow members would encourage me and let me know that I inspired them.

I had never felt that way before. I never believed that I could inspire someone else.

As time went on, I became stronger and faster. More importantly, CrossFit has shown me how strong I am mentally, emotionally and spiritually. Every workout has given me the opportunity to either give up or push for the man that I want to be. I have been able to participate in local competitions and have not been afraid to put myself in front of a crowd and show who I have become.

After two years of Crossfit, I am below 400 pounds for the first time in over 8 years. My mile time is at about 15:00 and my lifts are much stronger.

The best part, thanks to my coaches and friends, is that I am now who I am meant to be. I have not reached my goal by any means, but I know that I will get there.

As I continue to grow personally, my next goal is to start helping others that are at the place that I once was. I want to change lives. I recently got my Level 1 Certification and can now help others like myself find who they really are and I will use CrossFit as a platform to do this.

There are so many people that are hurting and don't believe in themselves. I cannot wait to see who the next changed life is, and I am humbled that I can be a part of it.

Get Involved

Do you have a story about how Functional Fitness has helped you get through a tough time in your life, or do you know someone else who has benefited from it?

We'd love to hear your story and share it with the world too.

Hope RX'd Volume 2 is scheduled to be released in 2016. If you would like your story to be considered for the next book, please visit http://www.hoperxd.com.

Story submission guidelines are provided for you to review before making a submission.

We look forward to hearing about your story!

Biography of Kelly Anne Graham

Kelly Graham was born in 1964 in a small Ontario town. She was always an active person, spending most of her childhood "hanging upside down in a tree". In fact, she credits a lot of her athletic success to being such an active and fearless child.

In high school, Kelly competed on every team offered by her tiny Catholic school, including volleyball, basketball, badminton, cross country running, and track and field.

She was a member of the Ontario Junior Women's Volleyball team, competing in the Canada Games held in Quebec in 1983. Kelly played varsity volleyball at the University of Toronto.

Shortly after graduation, Kelly married Edward Graham. They settled back in her hometown and raised 3 amazing children, Sarah, Carlie and Brett.

Kelly coached high school volleyball, basketball, track and field, badminton, soccer, girl's ice and ball hockey and cross country running. She was awarded the Ontario Federation of School Athletic Associations coach of the year for her development of the girl's ice hockey program.

During this time, Kelly became an avid ball hockey and ice hockey player, competing at the Provincial and National level. She continued to follow her love for volleyball and was a member of a team which dominated league play for over a decade. Kelly and her partner earned a 2nd place ranking in the province for women's beach volleyball. Kelly was inducted into the

Midland Sports Hall of Fame in 2002.

She and her husband have recently retired from careers in teaching.

It wasn't until late August 2011, that Kelly entered a CrossFit gym for the first time. She participated in The Open (a worldwide CrossFit competition) in February of 2012 and earned a 48th place ranking in the world in her master's category.

It was at this time that she set the goal to qualify for the CrossFit Games held in July of 2013. Kelly continued to train and developed a disciplined lifestyle and did in fact qualify as the oldest person in the women's 44-49 year old category.

At 49 years old, she earned a 10th place standing in the world at the end of the CrossFit Games. Knowing she would be entering a new category the following year as one of the youngest women, Kelly set her sites on the podium.

After qualifying for the 2014 Games, earning a 7th place ranking in the world, she experienced a serious injury in two cervical discs. This injury was just a day before the Eastern Canadian Regionals in which Kelly was to compete as a team member with *Driven Athletics*.

Unable to perform the movements due to extreme pain and weakness, she had to pull out of the competition and leave her team one person short and therefore unable to complete the workouts as prescribed.

This was a disappointment for all and the effect this had on others was not lost on Kelly. Her disc injuries were severe enough to cause the loss of muscle function and tone in some areas of her arm and back, and it has been a very painful and frustrating year.

Unable to compete at the Games was a difficult loss and prognosis for returning to competition has not been favourable, in fact some attending doctors advised against further training.

Kelly is the first to admit that she has so much

in her life to be grateful for, but is very honest about the process she needed to work through after this sudden change in her goals, her daily routines and her focus.

Two months after her injury, a friend brought her a book called *"The Success Principles"* written by Jack Canfield. After reading this book, Kelly was inspired to put to practice some key concepts and came up with the idea of creating her own motivational/inspirational book containing first hand accounts of people finding strength and hope through the functional fitness community.

She began by writing a post on her Facebook page, Kelly Graham-Athlete. Slowly stories started to come in. A few key individuals with an established internet presence saw her inquiry and posted articles about Kelly and her book.

Kelly was interviewed via Skype by the *Leading Ladies Company* for their web cast in England and this helped spread the word in Europe, which led to more stories coming in.

The final and most successful call for stories occurred when Kelly and her husband emailed close to a thousand functional fitness gyms around the world.

Today, Kelly is a trainer at ***Driven Athletics — Huronia CrossFit***.

She has been approached to be a motivational speaker at events with regard to picking up the pieces, moving forward and staying positive when life doesn't go as planned.

Kelly is so proud of the end result and thanks all contributors for trusting in her and this project.

Hope RX'D is the first book Kelly has created and it is the first in this series of inspirational books.

She encourages anyone with a story to share to contact her through her website: www.kellyannegraham.com or www.hoperxd.com.

Made in the USA
Middletown, DE
02 October 2015